Madame d' Aulnoy

The Ingenious and Diverting Letters of the Lady - Travels Into Spain

Describing the devotions, nunneries, humours, customs, laws, militia, trade, diet, and recreations of that people. Second Edition

Madame d' Aulnoy

The Ingenious and Diverting Letters of the Lady - Travels Into Spain
Describing the devotions, nunneries, humours, customs, laws, militia, trade, diet, and recreations of that people. Second Edition

ISBN/EAN: 9783337244569

Printed in Europe, USA, Canada, Australia, Japan

Cover: Foto ©Andreas Hilbeck / pixelio.de

More available books at **www.hansebooks.com**

Marie Catherine le Jumel de Barneville,
Baroness of Aulnoy

THE
Ingenious and Diverting
LETTERS
OF THE
Lady——Travels
INTO
SPAIN

DESCRIBING

The Devotions, Nunneries, Humours, Customs, Laws, Militia, Trade, Diet, and Recreations of that People.

Intermixt with

Great Variety of Modern Adventures, and Surprising Accidents: being the Truest and Best REMARKS Extant on that Court and Country.

The Second Edition

LONDON:

Printed for *Samuel Crouch*, at the Corner of *Pope's-Head-Alley*, next *Cornhil*. 1692.

G. P. Putnam's Sons
The Knickerbocker Press
New York & London

To
W. W. D.

Licenfed,

Sept. 2, 1691.

Rob. Midgley.

To the Honourable

Mʳˢ *Martha Lockhart*

MADAM,

I Humbly beg Leave thefe Letters may appear in an Englifh Drefs, under the Protection of your Name; whofe Accuracy in the Original, juftly Intitles you to this Dedication; and whofe Advantagious Birth, Greatnefs of Mind, and Uncommon Improvements, exact a Veneration from the moft Invidious; and render you an Illuftrious Ornament of your Sex.

Madam, For me to attempt here the Publifhing your Vertues

The Epistle Dedicatory

tues and Accomplishments, so universally acknowledg'd by all that have the Honour of your Acquaintance, would be to detract from your Merit; and might more justly be censured for Presumption than Flattery.

It were better to imitate the Painter, who perceiving it not possible to represent the Father's Grief for the loss of his Daughter, drew a Veil over his Face, and owned his Inability.

But I forget, Madam, 'tis my part only to crave your Pardon for this bold Address; and to study ever to approve myself,

Madam,

Your most Obedient Servant.

TO THE
READER

IT is not sufficient to write things true, but they muſt likewiſe ſeem probable, to gain belief. This has ſometime ſo prevail'd with me, as to make me think of retrenching from my Relation the ſtrange Stories you will find therein. But I have been withheld from doing this, by Perſons of ſuch great Sence and Merit, as has made me conclude, that I cannot do amiſs in following their Judgments.

I do not doubt but there will be ſome, who will accuſe me of hyperbolizing, and compoſ-
ing

To the Reader

ing Romances; but such would do well to acquaint themselves first with the Countrey, Humour, and Character of those I treat of. A Fact must not be presently condemn'd as false, because it is not publick, or may not hit every Man's Fancy. I cite no feigned Names, no Persons whose Death may give me the Liberty of attributing what I please to them.

In a word: I write nothing but what I have seen, or heard from Persons of Unquestionable Credit; And therefore shall conclude with assuring you, That you have here no Novel, or Story, devised at pleasure; but an Exact and most True Account of what I met with in my Travels.

CONTENTS

	PAGE
INTRODUCTION	XV
LETTER I	1
LETTER II	50
LETTER III	100
LETTER IV	148

ILLUSTRATIONS

	PAGE
Marie Catherine le Jumel de Barneville, Baroness of Aulnoy . . *Frontispiece.*	
Gateway of Fuenterrabia	46
A Town of Central Spain	100
Medina del Campo . . .	144

INTRODUCTION

AT the end of the seventeenth century and the beginning of the eighteenth there were several women in France who had gained no small reputation for the writing of amusing if somewhat extravagant *Contes des Fées*. Of these Marie-Catherine Le Jumel de Barneville, Baroness of Aulnoy, has best survived her contemporaries as the author of *La Chatte Blanche, La Grenouïlle Bien-complaisante, Le Prince Lutin, L'Oiseau Blèue*, and of other tales which, as M. La Harpe has thought, place her supreme in the realm of delicate frivolity.

The life of this brilliant woman will doubtless present a contrast with most preconceptions of her character based upon a mere reading of her books; and we may be surprised to find in her such a marked individuality, so peculiarly in touch with her time, and offering so little of the ideal and sensitive nature it was fairly natural to infer. We have not, in fact, a mere writer of amusing tales and half romantic histories, but an intriguing, though charming, woman, of a bold and often reckless nature, sufficient to stamp her a worthy daughter of her time. And, after all harsh verdicts have been passed, we shall, I think, return to Madame Aulnoy, by way of her books, with a feeling of affection and interest.

Barneville, near Bourg-Achard (Eure), is her birthplace. Her father was Nicolas-Claude Le Jumel, and her mother, who subsequently married the Marquis of Gudaigne and went with him to Rome, Judith-Angélique Le Coustellier. Nicolas is said to have served long in the armies of Louis XIV., and to have been related to some of the best families of Normandy. Judith later, when in Rome, seems to have rendered peculiar services to the Spanish court, for which she was duly rewarded.

The date of their daughter's birth is not positively fixed. It is given as 1650 or 1651, but no record of baptism remains, and of the life of Madame Aulnoy previous to the date of her marriage with François de La Motte little is known. That event occurred on Monday, the 8th of March, 1666.

But if the minor details of her life are wanting, we have yet a general and quite sufficient survey of its broader lines. Married at sixteen to a man thirty-six years her senior, we may find in the character of her husband (" un assez triste personage," as one of his biographers has named him) no uncertain commentary on the subsequent behavior of his wife.

He is described as: "Un bel homme, bien fait, d'abord valet de pied de César, duc de Vendôme, qui cherchait d'avoir de beaux hommes à son service."

He rose in the confidence of this master, who in 1649 to 1650 employed him in important affairs. This duke of Vendôme, called by Le Vassor* "un mince capitaine, que ne sut jamais se faire craindre ni se faire estimer," had, on his return to France in 1641, been accused of an attempt to poison Richelieu. These were the days of the celebrated Brinvilliers, when *Acqua Tofana* had been brought from Italy and the number of poisoners was increasing in France. The duke had again returned after the death of Richelieu, and under Mazarin in 1650 was given the government of Bourgogne. In 1653 he took Bordeaux, and two years later put to flight the Spanish fleet before Barcelona. It was in 1653 that La Motte, rising to prosperity with the fortunes of his master, was made Chevalier de Saint-Michel, and one year later he purchased for

* *Histoire de Louis XIII.*

150,000 livres from Claude Gobelin the Barony of Aulnoy in Brie. His success was, however, of short duration, and his money soon slipped away. He died in 1700 in his eightieth year, "Accablé de ses infortunes et des infamies de ses filles, dont il y en a deux qui imitent leur mère."

In view, therefore of the seemingly general evil opinion as to the character of François de La Motte we may possibly abate somewhat of the severity of judgment in regard to his wife. Yet on the whole Madame Aulnoy does not present a too pleasing portrait. Of her five children two only were acknowledged by their father. Marie-Angélique was born on the 26th of January, 1667 ; Dominique-César on the 22d of November of the same year ; Anne, 1668 ; Judith-Henriette, 1669 ; Thérèse-Aymée in 1676.

Of these the only son died young. Thérèse was taken to Spain in the early part of 1679 by Madame Aulnoy, whither the latter had gone to rejoin her mother, the Marquise de Gudaigne. Marie-Angélique, it appears, had the clever nature of her mother, and won a salon reputation. She married Claude Denis de Herre de Vaudois. Anne, the most beautiful, married a gentleman of Berry, by name M. de Preaulx d'Artigny. Thérèse-Aymée remained in Spain with the queen, where she was in 1705. Judith-Henriette seems to have remained in Paris and followed, in a "carrière d'intrigue et de galanterie," the footsteps of her mother and grandmother.

All amicable relations between Madame Aulnoy and her husband had come to an end even before the tragic event which all but involved her and her mother, and for which they were undoubtedly responsible. A certain C. Bonenfant, Seigneur de Lamoizière, and another, J. A. de Crux, Seigneur Marquis de Courboyer, who were, without seeming question, lovers of Madame Aulnoy and the Marquise de Gudaigne, attacked, at their instigation, in the courts, the unfortunate La Motte, who, however, managed to save himself, and the attempt ended in failure. The accusers were tried, put to the torture, and confessed. Both suffered death, and the two women found it necessary to make their escape. It was said that Madame Aulnoy was all but captured, having been found by the officer in bed, whence she managed to escape, and hid herself beneath a catafalque in a neighboring church. The two went first to England and afterwards to Spain. Here, however, having rendered some service to their own government, they were finally pardoned and returned to France, where, in 1699, Madame Aulnoy again appears, this time mixed up in the famous Ticquet scandal, which ended in the beheading of Angélique Ticquet on the 17th of June. Our author seems to have run some danger of joining her on the scaffold. She died, however, in her house in the Rue

Saint-Benoit on the 14th of January, 1705.

If the *Contes des Fées* of Madame Aulnoy have had a remarkable vogue, not so fortunate has been the lot of some of the historical endeavors of this lady. Her *Mémoires de la Cour d'Espagne* (1679–1681) and *Mémoires de la Cour d'Angleterre* (1695) have been quietly laid aside, together with the *Histoire d'Hippolyte, Comte de Douglas* (1690), and the *Histoire de Jean de Bourbon* (1692), for, though always interesting, the qualities of imagination which combine to the writing of a fairy tale are not quite those needed for the making of history, and unfortunately for the clever lady, it is in the field of "delicate frivolity" that she has been placed.

But Madame Aulnoy has put forward a more serious claim to legitimate reputation in the small volume of travel published anonymously at Paris in 1691, wherein she describes her voyage into Spain with a brilliancy and wealth of detail which is all the more grateful in that the period has furnished us with but little like it. In this Journey she has produced a remarkable book. To the quick eye of the clever French woman nothing is lost. She sees the astonishing condition of the Peninsula with an instant but not unsympathetic glance. Into what might have well proved a dismal picture she has woven her ever lively personality, and with a ready humor turns the incidents of evil chance to amusing asides. If in all this an air of unreality and lack of truth is introduced, it does not on the whole affect the picture. Nor does this resemble the more fanciful historical work of the same writer, for here at least all is natural and fairly told. Spaniards have been at pains to attack this writer. They have argued and abused. But it is not far wrong to find in her book a near approach to a truthful picture. There was, in fact, small need for calling up the imagination. There is evidence enough that in that day no one need closet himself and dream for the seeing of strange sights. It is the commonplace that surprises us. We feel how little the nation was responding to the sense of awakening which began to be felt elsewhere. Cervantes with his laughter had not brought to earth all fabrics of romance. The modern spirit was not yet stirring.

Of this book, as of Madame Aulnoy, Taine has been unhesitating in his praise. To him she was neither prude, philosopher, nor pedant; without affectation; a ready observer, praising or condemning with discretion, he seemed to find in her a representative in some measure of the great literary age of which she was a part.

And to him she never exaggerates; she has the inestimable qualities of good sense, frankness, and tact, is a French woman of culture and breeding. "On imprime," he says, speaking of the book before us, "beaucoup de livres nouveaux, on ferait bien de réimprimer quelques livres anciens, au premier rang celui-ci."

On the death of Philip IV., in 1665, a sigh of relief might well have risen from all Spain, yet scarcely through any anticipation of better days to come. For, though this man had presented to Europe a peculiarly marked type of bad government, his end raised no profound hopes of improvement. A man of strong character, of inflexible honesty, of patience; a statesman, a philosopher, and, last of all, a king, was what a few who remembered other days may have hoped. Instead, a Regency. At a time when throughout the land a magistrate, a viceroy, or a noble who had no place to sell or influence to buy was scarcely to be found; when an exhausted treasury, the loss of possessions, the slipping of prestige, the corruption of all classes, called for a guiding hand, then it was that fate saw fit to introduce a new king—*at the age of four*.

Spanish writers have a justified bitterness for this period of the national history. While the Imperial power was sinking slowly away, no return of prosperity, of New World conquest, or Old World grandeur appeared in the distance. None ever came. Stretching back into the past, the widening road of disaster ran straight to the foot of the throne of Philip II. On every side the downfall had begun. Spanish troops once invincible retreated and again retreated. Bit by bit the schemes of other countries began to be realized in the dismemberment of the Empire. Literature grown decadent, history perverted, Mannerism and Gongorism were the new gods and Churriguera the builder of their temples.

The arts decayed and died. Merchants, anticipating the destruction of trade, refused to venture their money. They rather hoarded it in secret places, discarding hope of interest. Commerce knew no security. Wealth brought but extortion. Power lay in the hands of court favorites.

"Les provinces étoient si épuisées," writes Villars, "qu'en quelques endroits de la Castille on étoit obligé pour vivre, de trocquer les marchandises, parcequ'il n'y avoit plus d'argent pour acheter. Dans Madrid même il ne se'en trouvoit presque plus, et l'on y ressentoit à loisir les suites du changement de la monnoye que l'on avoit fait, avec tant de précipitation. Les personnes de qualité dont la dépense avoit doublé par ce changement ne pouvoient payer leurs marchands, et les banquiers n'avoient plus de fonds et ne trouvoient point à emprunter ; on ne payoit rien dans la maison du Roy et les choses en vinrent à une telle extrémité, que la plus part des petits domestiques ayant rendu leurs livrées pour quitter le service, on eut beaucoup de peine à trouver les moyens de les y faire demeurer."

Even religion was to become the vehicle of a host of strange mysteries; professional saints flourished; miracles were of daily report, the stigmata had repeatedly appeared. Superstition fed upon tales of witches and hobgoblins, and the minds of high and low were filled with a strange, incongruous mass of belief and doubt. A whole supernatural world both local and national crowded the places of Christian tradition. Every fragment of Roman, Arabic, or Gothic belief came to be fused upon the general credulity.

While the form that faith had assumed no longer surprises the reader as he turns the pages of contemporary writers, yet the *auto de fé* had not gasped its last. Outside the gate of Fuencarral the fires still burned. In 1680, the very year in which our author is writing her later letters from Madrid, it had produced an exhibition in the Plaza Mayor which had the utmost detail of dramatic staging given it to lend impressiveness. The bullfight, too, was beginning to grow into that popularity which was later to make it the national sport.

The condition of the people was lamentable. Little by little the lower orders, driven from trades and manufacturing, were forced to face conditions of pauperism. Theft came to be too common to be noted. Every mountain pass was infested by robbers. People travelled well armed or stayed at home.

Into such a country, under such conditions as these, came, in February, 1679, this French woman of position, cultivation, and wit, and from San Sebastian she wrote the first of the series of letters which one by one found their way northward as she journeyed toward Madrid.

"Le premier trait du caractère Espagnol, c'est le manque de sense pratique," says Taine. Something, however, must be added to every epigram on Spain, for she will not permit of hasty summing. Something must be said of language, dignity, and, last but not least, of the instinctive ceremonial. All of this our author has perceived.

This ceremonial of Spain, what and whence is it and how is it that it is first discerned by the traveller? Its history, could it be written, would be indeed a history of shadows, a ghostly palimpsest of needs made forms. Time was when a stern and God-favored war, fought day by day, year to year, and century to century behind the Pyrenean wall, nursed and fostered strange forms and moulded fantastic mental attitude. Europe busied herself but little with it all. It was enough for her that the Spaniard did well his office of guard and watcher at the outer gate. There, she came to believe, was his place, and there he wore his livery. And a strange livery it was—made up of rags and tatters of Iberian pride, Roman servitude, and Christian independence, and as it was fought day after day at the cheerless outer gate, from time to time the foe who bore upon him with the banners of Islam fell back before him, leaving upon the field some word to be gathered up as booty, some spoil of solemn gesture or grave reply or strangely formed garment brought across all Africa from Hejaz or the land of the Anazeh. And in this strange attire he stood and fought and bled until with sweat and blood of a thousand years the garment was a single hue and had become a solemn cloak.

Then the word came for the sheathing of the sword to the south, and with this cloak wrapped about him the erstwhile guardian of the outer gate of a sudden stalked out upon Europe, jangling the gold purse of the Indies at his belt, to the terror and the unfeigned astonishment of the world.

And this strange, melancholy creation of spectral silence has worn his piecemeal cloak of historic ceremonial, and, like the garment of the Seises, when it grew too old and threadbare redarned and furbished it anew until it in turn became but a shade and figure of its predecessor, yet drawn ever closer and hugged with a dearer love about the wasting old guardsman's figure.

LETTERS
OF THE
Lady——Travels
INTO
SPAIN

A RELATION OF A Voyage to *SPAIN* IN Several Letters

LETTER I

SEEING you are so earnest with me to let you know all my Adventures, and whatever I have observ'd during my Travels, you must therefore be contented (my dear Cousin) to bear with a great many trifling Occurrences, before you can meet with what will please you: I know

your

your Fancy is fo nice and delicate, that none but extraordinary Accidents can entertain you ; and I wifh I had no others to relate: but recounting things faithfully, as they have hapned, you muft be contented therewith.

I gave you an Account in my laft, of what I met with as far as Bayonne: you know this is a Town in France, Frontier to Spain, wafh'd by the Rivers Dadour and Nivelle, which joyn together ; and the Sea comes up to them. The Port and Trade are confiderable: I came from Axe by Water, and obferv'd that the Boat-men of Adour have the fame Cuftom as thofe of Garonne ; which is to fay, That in paffing by one another, they fet up a Hollowing ; and they had rather lofe their Wages than to forbear these fort of Shoutings, although exceeding vexatious to thofe who are not ufed to them. There are two Caftles ftrong enough to defend the Town, and there are about it feveral pleafant Walks.

At

At my Arrival there, I intreated the Baron de Caſtlenau, who had accompany'd me from Axe, to bring me acquainted with ſome Women, with whom I might ſpend my time with leſs impatience, till the Litters came, which were to be ſent to me from St. Sebaſtian.

He readily complied with my Requeſt; for being a Perſon of Quality and Worth, he is much eſteem'd at Bayonne. He fail'd not the next Morning to bring ſeveral Ladies to viſit me.

Theſe Women begin here to feel the ſcorching Heats of the Sun; their Complexion is dark, their Eyes ſparkling; they are charming enough, their Wits are ſharp: And I could give you a farther Account of their Capacities, could I have better underſtood what they ſaid: not but that they could all ſpeak French, yet with ſuch a different Dialect, as ſurpaſt my Underſtanding.

Some who came to ſee me, brought
little

little Sucking Pigs under their Arms, as we do little Dogs: it's true they were very spruce, and several of 'em had Collars of Ribbons, of various Colours: However, this Custom looks very odd, and I cannot but think that several among themselves are disgusted at it: When they danced, they must set them down, and let these grunting Animals run about the Chamber, where they make a very pleasant Harmony. These Ladies danc'd at my Intreaty, the Baron of Castleneau having sent for Pipes and Tabors.

The Gentlemen who attended the Ladies, took each of 'em her whom he had brought with him, and the Dance began in a Round, all holding Hands: they had afterwards long Canes brought them, and then each Spark taking hold of his Lady's Handkerchief, which separated them from one another, moved very gracefully at the Sound of this Martial sort of Musick,

sick, which inspired them with such Heat, that they seem'd not to be able to moderate it. This seem'd to me to resemble the Pyrric Dance so much celebrated by the Ancients; for these Gentlemen and Ladies made so many Turns, Frisks and Capers, their Canes being thrown up into the Air, and dexterously caught again, that it is impossible to describe their Art and Agility: And I had a great deal of Pleasure in seeing 'em; but methoughts it lasted too long, and I began to grow weary of this ill-ordered Ball: When the Baron de Castleneau, who perceiv'd it, caused several Baskets of dried Fruit to be brought in. They are the Jews who pass for Portuguises, and dwell at Bayonne, who transport them from Genoa, and furnish all the Country with them. We wanted not for Limonade, and other refreshing Waters, of which these Ladies drank heartily; and so the Entertainment ended.

I was carry'd the next Morning to see the Synagogue of the Jews, in the Suburb of the Holy Spirit, but met with nothing remarkable there. Monsieur de St. Pe, the King's Lieutenant, who came to see me, though much troubled with the Gout, invited me to Dine at his House, where I was most deliciously entertain'd; for this a Country abounding with good Cheer, and at cheap Rates. I found here Women of Quality that were very handsome, whom he had invited to bear me Company. The sight of the Castle, which faces the River, is very pleasant, and has always a good Garison in it.

At my return to my Lodging, I was surpriz'd to find several Pieces of Linnen, which were brought to me from the Ladies who came to see me, with Baskets full of dried Sweetmeats. This Treatment seem'd to me very obliging to a Lady whom they had not known above four or five **Days.**

Days. But I must not forget to tell you, there is not any finer Linnen in the World, than that which is made in this Country, some of which is open like Net-work, and the Threads of it finer than Hair: And I remember, that travelling thro' the Villages of Bourdeaux, which may be rather call'd Desarts, the poor Peasants living so wretchedly; yet I found among them as neat Napkins as those used among People of Quality at Paris.

I fail'd not to send these Ladies such little Presents which I thought might please them: I perceiv'd they were great Admirers of Ribbons, and wear a great many on their Heads and Ears, which made me send them a great many; to which I added several Fans: and they, by way of Return, presented me with Gloves, and Thread-Stockins, most delicately knit.

In sending them to me they desired me to go to the next Chappel, which was not far from my Quarters, where they

they intended to Regale me with the beſt Muſick the Town would afford: but though there were very good Voices, yet there is no great pleaſure in hearing them, becauſe they want both Air and Skill.

The Litters which I expected from Spain, being come, I prepared for my Departure; but I never met with any thing dearer than theſe ſort of Equipages; for each Litter has a Maſter that accompanies it, who keeps the Gravity of a Roman Senator, being mounted on a Mule, and his Man on another, with which they releaſe ever and anon thoſe that carry the Litter. I had two, I took the greateſt for myſelf and my Child, and had beſides four Mules for my Servants, and two for my Baggage: to conduct them, there were other two Maſters and two Men. You ſee what Charge one is at, to go to Madrid, ſeeing you muſt pay not only for their Attendance on you forwards, but the ſame Price for
their

their return back: However, we muſt ſubmit to their Cuſtoms, and ſuffer ourſelves to be peel'd by them.

I found at Bayonne ſeveral Turks and Mores, and I think a worſe ſort of People, and theſe are Cuſtom-Houſe-Men: I had cauſed my Trunks to be weigh'd at Paris, that I might have the leſs to do with theſe ſort of People; but they were more ſubtle, or to ſpeak better, more obſtinate than I; ſo that I was forc'd to give them whatever they demanded. Scarcely was I got clear from them, when the Drums, Trumpets, Pipes, and Violins of the Town, came thundring upon me; they follow'd me farther than St. Anthony's Gate, through which you paſs for Spain through Biſcaye: they play'd each of them in their way, and all together, without any Harmony, which was enough to drive any one out of their Senſes: I ordered ſome Money to be given them, upon which they left

per-

perſecuting me. As ſoon as we had left Bayonne, we enter'd into a large barren Heath, where we ſaw nothing but Cheſnut-Trees; but we afterwards paſt along by the Sea, whoſe Sand makes a delightful Way, and a pleaſant Proſpect.

We arriv'd in good time at St. John de Luz: nothing can be pleaſanter than this Borough, which is the greateſt in France, and the beſt built; there are ſeveral ſmaller Cities: its Port lies between two Mountains, which Nature ſeems to have expreſly placed to defend it from Storms; the River Nivelle diſgorges it ſelf therein; the Sea comes up very high in it, and the greateſt Barks come up commodiouſly to the Key. The Seamen here are very skilful at catching Whales, and other large Fiſh. We were here very well entertain'd, ſo that our Tables were covered with all ſorts of Wild Fowl: but our Beds were not anſwerable, being ſtuck with Feathers whoſe
Pinions

Pinions ran into our fides, and we wanted Quilts to lay on the top of them: I thought when we were to pay, that we fhould have had a large Reckoning, but they only demanded of me half a Lewis Dor, when they would have coft more than five Piftoles at Paris. The Situation of St. John de Luz is extreamly agreeable.

In the moft fpacious part of the Town you fee here a very fine Church, built after the Modern Fafhion; and here is a Paffage over the River Nivelle, on a Woodden Bridge of great length. Here are Toll-Gatherers, who make you pay for every thing you carry with you, not excepting your Cloaths: This Tax is demanded at their Pleafure; and it is exceffive on Strangers. I was weary with fpeaking French to 'em, and protefting I was no Spaniard; they feigning not to underftand me, fneering in my Face, and wrapping up their Heads in their Hooded-Gowns; they feem'd to to be Thieves, difguifed in Capuchins: In fhort, they tax'd me eighteen Crowns, and would perfwade me they ufed me well, tho' I found the contrary. But I have already told you (dear Coufin), that when you travel this Country, you muft ftock yourfelf with Patience, and good ftore of Money.

I faw the Caftle of Artois, which feems a ftrong place; and a little farther Orognes, where the Bifcaye is fpoken, without either French or Spanifh. I defign'd to lye at Iron, which is but three Leagues diftant from St. John de Luz; and I had fet out after Noon, but the Difpute which we had with the Watch on the Bridge, the Difficulty we had in paffing the Mountains of Beotia, and the ill Weather, joyned to other little Difficulties which hapned, were the Caufe that it was Night before we arriv'd on the Borders of the River Bidaffoa, which feparates France from Spain.

Spain. I obferv'd along the way from Bayonne thither, little Carriages, on which they tranfport every thing, which have only two Iron Wheels, and the Noife they make is fo great, that they are heard a Mile off, when there are many of them together, which often happen; for you often meet with Sixty or Seventy at a time; they are drawn by Oxen. I have feen the fame in the Villages of Bourdeaux, and efpecially on the fide of Axe.

The River of Bidaffoa is ufually very fmall, but the Snows melting had increas'd it to fuch a degree, that we had no fmall trouble to pafs it, fome in a Boat, and others fwimming on their Mules: The Moon fhined very bright, by means of which I was fhew'd on the right Hand the Ifle of Conference, where the Marriage of our King was made with Maria Therefe, Infanta of Spain. I faw a while after the Fort of Fontarabia, which belongs to the King of Spain, ftanding on the

Mouth

Mouth of this small River: the Flux and Reflux of the Sea arrives here. Our Kings heretofore pretended it belonged to them: there have been such great Contests hereupon, especially by the Inhabitants of Fontarabia, and those of Andaye, that they have several times come to Blows. This oblig'd Lewis the Twelfth, and Ferdinand, to agree, That it should be common to both Nations: the French and the Spaniards take Toll equally; these last making those pay who pass into Spain, and the former doing the like in relation to those who pass over to France.

War does not hinder Commerce on this Frontier: it's true they cannot subsist without it, seeing they must perish through Want, did they not assist one another.

This Country call'd Biscaye, is full of high Mountains, where are several Iron Mines: The Biscays climb up the Rocks as easily, and with as great swift-

swiftness as Stags: Their Language (if one may call such Jargon Language) is very poor, seeing one Word signifies abundance of Things: There are none but those born in the Country that can understand it; and I am told, that to the end it may be more particularly theirs, they make no use of it in Writing; they make their Children to read and write French and Spanish, according to which King's Subjects they are. It's certain, as soon as I past the little River of Bidassoa, I was not understood, unless I spake Castillan; and not above a quarter of an Hour before, I should not have been understood had I not spoke French.

I found on the other side of this River a Banker of St. Sebastian, to whom I was recommended: he tarried for me, with two of his Relations; they were cloath'd after the French manner, but ridiculously, their Justau Corps being short and large, and their Sleeves hanging down very short;
those

thofe of their Shirts were fo large, that they hung down below their Juftau Corps: they had Bands without Collars; Periwigs, one of which had enough Hair for four, and fo frizled, as made 'em look as if they were frighted; iller-dreft People you cannot meet with. Thofe who wear their own Hair, wear it very long and clofe, parting it on the Crown, and pafs part of it behind their Ears: but what kind of Ears think you? thofe of Midas were not larger; and I believe, that to lengthen them, they are ftretched when they be young: without queftion they find fome kind of Beauty herein.

My three Spaniards made me in bad French moft tedious and dull Complements. We paft through the Bourg of Tran, which is about a quarter of a League from the River, and came afterwards to Irun, which is diftant about another quarter of a League: this little Town is the firft of
Spain

Spain which you meet with, leaving France: it's ill built; the Streets are unequal, and there's nothing one can speak of: We entered into the Inn through the Stable, where are the Stairs on which you must ascend to your Chamber; this is the Country's Fashion. I found the House very light, by a great many Candles, which were as small as Pack-thread; there were at least forty in my Chamber, fixt on little bits of Wood; in the midst of 'em stood a Pan of Coals burning, made of Olive Rhines, to take away the scent of the Candles.

I had a great Supper, which my Gallants, the Spaniards, had caus'd to be made ready for me; but all was so full of Garlick, Saffron and Spice, that I could eat nothing: and I had made very bad Cheer, had not my Cook made me a little Ragou of what he could find.

Determining to go but to St. Sebastian the next Morning, which is but
seven

seven or eight Leagues, I thought to Dine before I set out: I was sitting at Table when one of my Women brought me my Watch to wind it up, as it was my Custom at Noon; It was a striking Watch, of Tompion's make, and cost me fifty Lewises: My Banker, who was by me, shew'd some desire to see it; I gave it him, with a customary Civility. This was enough: my Blade rises, makes me a profound Reverence, telling me, "He did not deserve so considerable a Present; but such a Lady as I could make no other: That he would engage his Faith and Reputation, that he would never part with my Watch as long as he liv'd; and that he found himself extreamly oblig'd to me." He kist it at the end of his pleasant Complement, and thrust it into his Pocket, which was deeper than a Sack. You'll take me to be a very great Sot, in saying nothing to all this, and I do not wonder at it; but I confess ingenuously, I was so
surpriz'd

surpriz'd at his Proceeding, that the Watch was out of sight before I could resolve on what I was to do. My Women, and the rest of my Servants who were about me, stared on me, and I on them, blushing with Shame and Vexation to be thus caught: However, I recollected myself, and considered, that this Man was to pay me a good round Sum of Money for the Charge of my Journey, and to return Money to Bourdeaux, where I had taken it up; that having Bills of Credit on him, he might use several Tricks to me, and Put-offs, which might make me spend twice the Value of the Watch: In fine, I let him part with it, and endeavour'd to do myself Honour from a thing which gave me great Mortification.

I have learnt, since this little Adventure, that 'tis the Custom in Spain, when any thing is presented to one, if he likes it, and kisses your Hand, he may take it with him. This is a
very

very pleafant Fafhion, and being fufficiently acquainted with it, 'twill be my Fault if I am Trapt again.

I left this Inn where they peel'd me fufficiently; for this is a grievous dear Country, and every one ftrives to be Rich at his Neighbour's Coft. A while after we had left the Town we entred on the Pyrenean Mountains, which are fo high and fteep, that looking down, you fee, not without Horror, the Precipices which environ them; we went thus as far as Rentery: Don Antonio (which was my Banker's Name) went before me, and for my more commodious Paffage, he oblig'd me to quit my Litter; for although we had traverft feveral Mountains, yet there remain'd more difficult to pafs: he made me enter into a little Boat, which he had prepar'd to go down the River of Andaye, till we were near the Mouth of the Sea, where we saw the King of Spain's Gallions; there were three
very

very fine and large ones. Our little boats were set forth with Gilt Streamers; they were manag'd by Girls, who were very lusty and handsome; there are three in each, two that Row, and one who holds the Rudder.

These Wenches are very well shaped, of Chesnut Complexion, have very good Teeth, Hair Black, which they tie up with Ribbons, in Knots, and so let it hang behind them: They wear a kind of Veil on their Heads, made of Musling, embroidered with Flowers of Gold and Silk, which hangs loose, and covers their Breasts: they wear Pendants in their Ears of Gold and Pearls, and Bracelets of Coral; they have a kind of Justau Corps, like our Gypsies, whose Sleeves are very strait: I can assure you they charm'd me. I was told these Wenches swim like Fishes, and suffer neither Women nor Men among them. This is a kind of Republick, where they repair from all Parts, and
where

where their Parents fend them very young.

When they are willing to marry, they go to Mafs at Fontarabia, which is the neareft Town to 'em; and there the young Men come to chufe 'em Wives to their Humour. He that will engage himfelf in Hymen's Bonds, goes to his Miftrefs's Parents, declares to them his Intentions, regulates every thing with them: And this being done, notice of it is given to the Maid: If fhe likes the Party, fhe retires to their houfe, where the Nuptuals are celebrated.

I never faw a more gay Air than that on their Countenances; they have little Habitations along the Waterfide, and there are old Maidens to whom the younger pay Refpect, as to their Mothers. They related thefe Particulars to us in their Language, and we hearken'd to 'em with great Delight, when the Devil, who never fleeps, difturb'd us with a vexatious Adventure.

My

My Cook, who is a Gascon, and exactly of the Humour of those of that Country, was in one of our Boats behind us, at some distance, very near a young Biscaneer, who appeared to him very handsome; he contented not himself with telling her as much, but would have rudely turn'd up her Veil. She being not used to this sort of plain Dealing without any Words broke his Head with her Oar: Having done this Exploit, Fear seizing on her, she threw herself immediately into the Water, tho' the Season was very cold, and swam with great swiftness; but having all her Cloaths on, and it being far to the Shoar, her strength began to fail her. Several of these Wenches who saw this at Land, leapt immediately into their Boats to her Assistance, when those who had remain'd in the Boat with the Cook, fearing the loss of their Companion, fell on him like two Furies, resolving by all means to drown him, and had like

two

two or three times to have overturn'd their little Veffel, which we beholding from ours, had much a-do to part and appeafe them.

I affure you the foolifh Gafcon was fo cruelly handled, that he was all over blood; and my Banker told me, that thefe young Bifcaneers provoked, are worfe than Lions. In fine, we came to Land, but were fcarcely on Shoar, but we faw this Wench which was faved out of the Water, making up towards us, with near fifty others, each with an Oar on their Shoulder, marching in Battle-ray, with Fife and Drum; when fhe who was to be the Mouth of the Company, advanc'd, and calling me feveral times Andria, which is to fay, Madam, (for that's all I could retain of her Speech) gave me to underftand, That they would have my Cook's Skin, if Satisfaction were not made proportionably to the Damage done their Companion's Cloaths. At the ending of which words, the
She-

She-Drummers fell loudly beating their Drums, and the reſt of their Amazons ſet up an Hollowing, Leaping and Dancing, and Fencing with their Oars in a moſt aſtoniſhing manner.

Don Antonio, to make me amends for the Preſent he had wrung from me (I cannot but óften mention it, lying on my Heart as it does) undertook to make Peace: He found that my Cook, who thought himſelf ſufficiently beaten, had Reaſon to give nothing; and therefore he diſtributed ſome Pieces of Money among this Marine Troop: On receipt of which they ſet forth lowder Hollow's than before, and wiſh'd me a good Journey, and ſpeedy Return, each of 'em dancing and ſinging at the ſound of their Pipes and Tabors.

We entred into a very rough Way, and aſcended along very narrow Paths, on the ſide of which there are Precipices; ſo that I was greatly afraid, leſt the Mules which carry'd my Litter
ſhould

should stumble: We afterwards past over a large Sandy Field. I tarry'd some time in the Convent of St. Francis, which stands near the River of Andaye: We past over it on a very long Wooden Bridge; and though we were very near St. Sebastian, yet we could not then perceive it, because a Mount of Sand hid the Town: It's situated on the Foot of a Mountain, which serves on one side as a Rampart against the Sea, and the Vessels come to the Foot of this Mountain, to shelter them from the Storms; for here arise extraordinary Tempests, that the Ships at Anchor perish in the Port: it's deep, and defended by two Moles, which leave only as much room as is requisite for one Vessel passing at a time. They have rais'd here a great four Square Tower, where there is ever a good Garison to defend the Place, in case of Assault: it was a fine Day for the Season: I found the Town very pleasant, being
fur-

surrounded with a double Wall: there are mounted several Pieces of Cannon on that part towards the Sea, with Bastions and Half Moons: the Town is situated in a Province of Spain, call'd Guipuscoa: the Outparts are exceeding pleasant, by reason that the Sea, as I now said, serves for a Channel to it: the Streets of this Town are long and large, pav'd with great White Stones, which are always clean: the Houses are well enough; and the Churches decent, in which the Altars are of Wood, on which are hung little Pictures, from top to bottom. Mines of Iron and Steel abound in this Country, finer and purer perhaps than in any other Parts of Europe; and this is the greatest part of their Trade. Here the Wool which comes from Castille, is embark'd, which makes a considerable part of their Traffick. Bilbo and St. Sebastian are two of the most considerable Ports which the King of Spain has

has on the Ocean: The Castle stands very high, and may make an indifferent Defence: here are mounted several fine Pieces of Cannon; and there are a great many along the Ramparts; but the Garison is so weak, that the Women might conquer them with their Distaffs.

Every thing is as dear in this Town as in Paris, yet they fare well here: Fish is excellent, and I was told Fruit was the same. I lay in the best Inn, and when I had been there some time, Don Fernand de Toledo, sent his Gentlemen to enquire, Whether his Visit would not be troublesome to me? My Banker, who knew him, and who was then in my Chamber, told me, he was a Spaniard of great Quality, Nephew to the Duke D' Alva; that he came from Flanders, and was going to Madrid.

I receiv'd him with that Civility which was due to his Birth, and soon thereto adjoyn'd particular Respects to to his own Merit: He is a Gentleman of good Prefence, has Wit and Politenefs, is Complaifant and Agreeable; he fpeaks as good French as I do; but underftanding Spanifh, and being defirous to fpeak it better, we therefore difcours'd only in that Language.

I was very well fatisfied with his Carriage. He told me he came Poft hither from Bruffels, and if I pleas'd, he would increafe my Train, and be one of my Company. I thought he jefted, and anfwered him accordingly; but he added, The ways were fo full of Snow, that indeed they could not ride Poft; that he could make more fpeed on Horfes than in Litters, but the Honour of accompanying me, made a bundant Recompence for that. In a word, I faw he was a civil Perfon, and came no way fhort of the Gallantry natural to the Spanifh Cavaliers: I therefore confider'd, how advantageous it might prove to have a Man of this Quality, and Country, who could
make

make himself be heard and obey'd by the Muletteers, who have Iron Souls, and no Confciences.

I told him, I was very glad I met with him, and the Fatigue of the Road would be lefs'ned by his Company. He immediately thereupon ordered his Gentlemen to find a Litter for him: It being late he took his leave of me, and I betook my felf to be after a good Supper; for, my dear Coufin, I am none of thofe Romantick Ladies that never eat.

Scarcely did I begin to fleep, when I heard fome-body fpeak French fo near me, that I thought at firft 'twas in my Chamber; but having hearkned with more attention, I found 'twas in a Chamber feparated from mine by only fome thin Boards, and thofe ill joynted: I drew my Curtain, and faw Light through the Crevices, and at the fame time two young Women, the eldeft of which appeared not to be above Seventeen or Eighteen; neither

neither of 'em were of thofe Beauties without Defect, yet were they fo pretty, fpake fo fweetly, and had fuch great fweetnefs on their Countenances, that I was much taken with 'em.

The youngeſt, who feem'd to continue the Converfation, faid to the other, 'No, my dear Sifter, there is no Remedy to our Misfortunes; we muſt die, or get them out of the Clutches of this vilanous Dotard.' 'I am refolute for any thing,' reply'd the other, in uttering a deep figh, 'fhould it coft me my Life: What remains? Have we not facrific'd all for them?' Then confidering a while their Misfortunes, they mutually embrac'd, and began to weep in a moſt piteous manner: And having confulted a while, and fpake fome other Words, the greateſt part of which were interrupted by their Sighs, they concluded on Writing, which they did; and here is moſt of what I heard them read to one another:

'Judge

'Judge not of my Love and Grief by my Words, I have none can exprefs either the one or the other; but remember you Ruine me, unlefs you betake yourfelf to the greateft Extremities againft him that perfecutes us. He has now fent me word, That if we delay our Departure, he will have us feiz'd. Confider what he deferves from this bafe Ufage of us; and remember you owe me all, feeing you owe me my Heart.'

I think the other Billet was in thefe Terms:

'Could I fecure thee thy Happinefs, in lofing mine, I love thee fufficiently to offer thee fuch a Sacrifice: Yes, I would fly from thee, couldft thou be Happy without me; but I know thy Heart too well to believe this. Yet thou remaineft as Quiet in thy Prifon, as if I were with thee: Break thy Chains without more delay; punifh the Enemy of our Loves. My Heart fhall be thy Recompenfe.'

Having

Having made up thefe Billets, they went out together; and, I profefs, I was not a little uneafie for 'em, and no lefs curious to know thefe poor Ladies Misfortunes. This hindred me from fleeping, and I was expecting their Return, when immediately there was a great Uproar in the Houfe: I faw an old Man enter the Chamber, attended by a great many Servants: He held one of thefe young Women by the Hair of the Head, which he had wound about his Arm, and drew her after him, as a wretched Sacrifice. Her Sifter was not treated with lefs Cruelty, by thofe who led her: 'Perfidious Wretches,' faid he to them, 'not content with the irreparable Injury you do my Nephews, you would perfwade them to be my Executioners? Had I not furprifed you with thefe feducing Letters, what might have hapned? What dreadful Tragedies might I not have expected? But you fhall pay once for all: as foon

as

as ever the Day appears I will have you punisht as you deserve.' 'Ah Sir,' said she whom he held, 'remember we are Women of Quality, and that our Alliance can be no Dishonour to you; that your Nephews have given us their Faith, and we them ours; that in so tender an Age we have left all for their sakes; that we are Strangers, and have no Friends here: What will become of us? We dare not return to our Relations: if you are for constraining us to this, or for putting us in Prison, let us intreat you rather presently to dispatch us out of the World.'

The Tears which they shed in such abundance, wrought in me the greatest Compassion: And had the old Man been as tender as I, he had soon freed 'em from their Trouble.

My Women, who had heard such a great Disturbance, and so near my Chamber, arose, in the fear of some Mishap towards me: I made Signs to them

them to draw near foftly, and to behold through the Boards this forrowful Spectacle: We hearkned to what they faid, when two Men, with their Swords in their Hands, entred into my Chamber, the Door of which my Women had left open: They had Defpair painted on their Faces, and Rage in their Eyes: I was fo greatly frighted, that I cannot exprefs it to you. They lookt on one another without fpeaking a word; and having heard the old Man's Voice, they ran on that fide.

I did not doubt but 'twas the two Lovers; and 'twas them indeed, who entred like two Lions into this Chamber: They ftruck thefe Servants with fo great Terror, that never a one of 'em dared approach his Mafter, to defend him, when his Nephews advance towards him, and fet their Swords to his Throat: 'Barbarian,' faid they to him, 'can you thus ufe Women of Quality, that are to be our Wives?

Wives? Becaufe you are our Guardian, muft you therefore be our Tyrant? And is not the feparating of us from what we love, the taking our Lives from us? It's now in our Power to take a juft Vengeance of you; but we cannot do it to a Man of your Age, who cannot defend himfelf: give us then your Word, and fwear by all that's Good and Holy, That in Acknowledgment for the Life we give you, you will contribute to our Happinefs, and fuffer us to perform what we have promis'd.'

The poor old Wret[c]h was fo afrighted, that he could hardly make any Anfwer: However, he fwore more than they would have him; he fell on his Knees, and kift an hundred times his Thumb laid a-crofs one of his Fingers, after the manner of Spain. Yet he told them, 'That whatever he had done, was onely in regard to their Interefts; however, he would not in any fort, for the future, oppofe their
Incli-

Inclinations, in reference to this Marriage.' Two of the Domesticks took him under the Arm, and rather carried him away than led him. Then the Gentlemen seeing themselves free, threw themselves in their Mistresses Arms; they said to one another, whatever Grief, Love and Joy do usually inspire in such Occasions. But in Troth, one must have a Heart as affected and content as theirs, to repeat all these things: they are only proper to Persons more tender than you are, my dear Cousin. But I hope you will excuse this Relation; I was so tired, in having not yet slept, that I could scarce hear any more, but confusedly: and to hear no more, I got farther into Bed, and threw the Quilt over my Head.

The next Morning Don Fernand de Toledo, sent me some choice Wines, with great quantity of Oranges and Sweetmeats. As soon as he thought it a proper time to Visit me, he came:
Having

Having thankt him for his Prefent, I askt him, Whether he had heard nothing of what had paft in the Night? He told me, No; for he had lain in another part of the Houfe. I was about relating to him what I knew, when our Hoftefs entred into the Chamber: fhe came from the two Gentlemen who had given me that Difturbance, with the Swords in their Hands, intreating me to receive their Excufes. She likewife told me, That two young Ladies defired they might wait on me, and kifs my Hand. I anfwered thefe Civilities as I ought; and they foon entred.

What charming Effects does the Return of Joy produce? I found thefe Gentlemen very well fhaped, and thefe Ladies very lovely; neither one nor the other had any more on their Countenances the Characters of Defpair; an Air of Gaiety difplay'd itfelf in all their Words and Geftures. The Eldeft of the two Brethren made the moft moſt handſome Excuſe as is poſſible for his Miſtake in entring my Chamber: he added, 'He had well obſerv'd the Fear he had caus'd me; but told me, that in that Moment he was ſo tranſported, that he was capable of no other Thought but the Reſcuing his Miſtreſs.' 'You would have been to blame,' ſaid I to him, 'ſhould you have thought of any thing elſe: However, if it be true, you are willing to make me Satisfaction for the Alarum you have giv'n me, you muſt not refuſe the gratifying my Curioſity: With theſe fair Ladies leave, inform me what has reduced all of you to theſe Extremities you were in.' He lookt on them, as if it were to ask their Approbation, which they willingly granted; and he thus began:

'We are two Brothers, Madam, Natives of Burgos, and of one of the beſt Families of this City. We were very young, when we fell into the Hands of an Uncle, who took care of

our

our Education and Estates, which are so considerable, that we need not envy others on that account; Don Diego (is our Uncle's Name) he had made long since a firm Friendship with a Gentleman living near Blaye, whose Merit is far above his Fortune; he is call'd Monsieur de Mesignac: our Uncle resolving to send us for some time into France, he wrote hereupon to his Friend, who offered him his House, which he joyfully accepted. He made us set out; and it is a Year since we were received there with great Civility: Madam de Messignac used us as her own Children; she has several; but of her four Daughters, those you see are the most aimable. It would have been very difficult to have seen them every day, to dwell with them, and yet not to have loved them.

'My Brother at first conceal'd from me his growing Passion, and I hid mine from him; we were both of us
very

very melancholly; the trouble of loving, without being lov'd again, and the fear of displeasing those who caus'd our Passion, all this cruelly tormented us; but a new Vexation did greatly increase our Disquiet, which was a restless Jealousie we had one of another: My Brother plainly saw I was in Love, and thought 'twas with his Mistress; I lookt on him likewise as my Rival; and we bore such Hatred to one another, as might have transported us to the greatest Extremities; but that I resolutely determin'd one day to discover my Sentiments to Mademoiselle de Messignac; but wanting Courage to speak to her myself, I wrote some Verses in a little Book touching my Passion for her, and dexterously slid it into her Pocket, without her perceiving me. My Brother, who had always an Eye on me, observ'd it, and playing with her, he took out the Verses, and found 'em to contain a respectful and passionate Declaration

of

of Love to her; he kept them till Night, when being withdrawn into my Chamber, with the greateſt Inquietude, he came to me, and tenderly embracing me, he told me, He was heartily glad at the notice he had of my being in love with Mademoiſelle de Meſſignac.

'I remain'd as one Thunderſtruck; I ſaw my Papers in his Hands; I imagin'd ſhe had made them a Sacrifice to him, and that he came to inſult on my Misfortune. He ſaw in my Eyes and Countenance part of what I thought: "Undeceive yourſelf," continued he, "ſhe gave 'em not to me; I have taken 'em without her ſeeing them: I'll be ſerviceable to you for the obtaining her; be you the ſame to me in relation to her elder Siſter." I then embraced him, and promis'd him all he deſired. Then we mutually rendred good Offices to one another; and our Miſtreſſes, who were not then acquainted with the power of
Love,

Love, began to accuftom themfelves to hear talk of it.

'It would be to abufe your Patience, to tell you, Madam, how we came at length by our Cares and Affiduities to win their Hearts. What happy Moments! what fweet Hours! to fee without ceafing what one loves, and to be beloved! to be together in the Fields, where an Innocent and Country Life let's one tafte, without difturbance, the Pleafures of a growing Paffion; this is a Felicity which cannot be expreft.

'Winter being come, Madam de Meffignac was at Bourdeaux, where fhe had a Houfe; we accompanied her thither; but this Houfe was not great enough to lodge us, with all our Family; we took one near hers.

'Though this Separation was only the Nights, yet we had lively Refentments of it; we were not now every Moment with 'em; our Vifits were accompanied with a certain Air of

Cere-

Ceremonies, which disturb'd us. But our Alarums were much increas'd when we saw two rich handsome Sparks address themselves to Mademoiselles de Messignac, and earnestly Court them, and that with the Approbation of their Parents. Good God, how we lookt! Their Proceedings went on at a great rate, and our dear Mistresses, who shared in our Sorrow, mingled every day their Tears with ours. In fine, having thoroughly tormented ourselves, by devising a thousand fruitless Ways, I resolv'd to Address myself to Monsieur de Messignac: I spake to him, and told him what my Passion inspired me, to perswade him to defer these Marriages. He answer'd, "He accepted, with the greatest Acknowledgments, the Offers my Brother and I made him; but being not of Age, what we might do at present might be afterwards Cancell'd: That his Honour was dear to him, though his Estate was small; however, should

should always esteem himself Happy, in living without Reproach: That my Uncle, who had entrusted us to him, might justly accuse him of Seducing us; and that in short, we must no more think of these matters."

'I withdrew in the greatest Affliction, which I shared with my Brother; and this was a dreadful trouble among us. Monsieur de Messignac, to compleat our misfortunes, sent an Account to my uncle, of what had past, and earnestly intreated him to lay his Commands on us to be gone. He did so; and seeing no remedy to our Misfortune, we went, my Brother and I, to Mademoiselles de Messignac, we threw ourselves at their Feet; We told them what might perswade Hearts already pre-possest: We gave them our Faith, and Promises, Sign'd with our Blood: In short, Love made an end of vanquishing them; they consented to go with us. In fine, we took such Measures, that our

Passage

Paſſage was happy enough till our Arrival here; and it is not two days ſince entring this Houſe, the firſt Perſon offering himſelf to us was Don Diego; He was impatient of our Return; and to ſatisfie himſelf, he came in queſt of us. How did we look at this ſight! He caus'd us to be apprehended as Criminals; and forgetting that Mademoiſelles de Meſſignac were the Daughters of his beſt Friend and Perſon of Quality, he loaded them with Injuries, and o'er-whelm'd them with Threatnings, after he had learnt from one of my Servants, that we had reſolved to paſs Incognito as far as Madrid, to ſome Relations we had there, to tarry in this place for a full liberty of declaring our Marriage. He lock't us up in a Chamber next to his; and we were there, when theſe Ladies came by Moon-light, coughing under our Windows. We heard them, and ran to them——They ſhew'd us their Letters; and we were deviſing on our
Deliv-

Gateway of Fuenterrabia

Deliverance, when my Uncle, having notice of what paſt, ſilently came upon us with all his Servants, and before our Faces miſuſed theſe aimable Creatures. In the Exceſs of our Deſpair our Strength, without doubt, increas'd; We broke open the Doors, which were faſt ſhut on us, and we ran to Succour them, when imprudently, Madam, we came into your Chamber.'

The Gentleman here ſtopt, and I found he had related his little Hiſtory with great Ingenuity. I thank't him for it, and offer'd theſe Ladies my Endeavours, and thoſe of my Friends, to appeaſe their Family: Which Offers they accepted, and teſtifi'd their Acknowledgments.

Some Ladies of the Town, who came to ſee me, wou'd ſtop me; they propoſed to me to go to the Religioſes, whoſe Convent is ſo pleaſantly situated, that the Proſpect has no Bounds: You may ſee thence, at the ſame time,

the

the Sea, Ships, Towns, Woods and Fields. They fpake much in praife of the Voices, Beauty, and good Humour of thefe Religiofes. Add to this, that the ill Weather was fo increaft, and the Snow fal'n in fo great abundance, that no body advifed me to proceed in my Journey. I was in fufpence a while, but the Impatience I had to be at Madrid, prevail'd over all thefe Confiderations, and I parted the next Morning. I have receiv'd of my Banker the Money I want.

But I muft not forget to tell you, That the Inhabitants of this Town have a particular Priviledge, and of which they are not a little proud; which is, That when they Treat of any Affairs with the King of Spain, and that it is directly with him, he is oblig'd to fpeak with them bareheaded. I could not get the Reafon from 'em for this.

I am told I muft furnifh myfelf with good ftore of Provifion, to prevent ftarvstarving in some places through which we must pass; and Gammons of Bacon, dried Tongues, being much esteem'd in this Country, I have therefore taken up a good quantity; and as to the rest, we have sufficiently provided. Now this being the Post-day, I would not omit this occasion of informing you of what has hapned to me; and testifying, that I am,

Yours.

From St. Sebastian,
   Feb. 20, 1679.

Letter II

I Re-affume, Dear Coufin, without any Compliments, the Sequel of my Travels: In leaving St. Sebaftian, we entred into a very rough Way, which brings you to fuch terrible fteep Mountains, that you cannot afcend them without climbing; they are call'd Sierra de St. Adrian. They fhew only Precipices and Rocks, on which a puling Lover may meet with certain Death, if he has a mind to it. Pine Trees of an extraordinary heighth crown the top of thefe Mountains. As far as the Sight will reach you fee nothing but Defarts, cut with Streams clearer than Chryftal. Near the higheft part of Mount St. Adrian, you meet with an elevated Rock, which feems to have been placed in the midft of the way

way to block up the Paſſage, and thus ſeparate Biſcaye from the Old Caſtille.

A tedious and painful Labour has pierced this Maſs of Stone in manner of a Vault; you may walk forty or fifty Paces under it, without ſight of Day, but what comes by the Overtures at each Entry, which are ſhut by great Doors: You find under this Vault an Inn, which is left in the Winter, by Reaſon of the Snows: You ſee here likewiſe a little Chappel of St. Adrian, and ſeveral Caverns, where Thieves commonly retreat; ſo that it is dangerous paſſing here without being in a condition of Defence. When we* had traverſt the Rock, we ſtill a little aſcended, to arrive to the top of the Mountain, which is held to be the higheſt of the Pyranea's; it is wholly covered with great Aſh Trees. There was never a finer place of Solitude; the Springs run here as in the Vallies: the ſight is only bounded by the

Weak-

* *Orig.* he.

Weakness of the Eyes; Shades and Silence here reign, and the Eccho's anſwers on every ſide. We began afterwards to deſcend down faſter than we climed up: We ſaw in ſome parts little barren Plains, many ſandy places, and ever and anon Mountains covered with great Rocks. It is not without Reaſon, that in paſſing ſo near, you fear, leſt ſome one of 'em ſhould get looſe, which would certainly over-whelm one; for you ſee ſome which are fall'n from the top, and hang in their paſſage on other Clefts; and theſe finding nothing in the way, would give a ſorry Diverſion to a Traveller. I made all theſe Reflections at my eaſe; for I was alone in my Litter, with my Child, who did not at all diſturb my Thoughts. A River call'd Urrola, big enough, but which was increaſed by the Torrents, and melted Snow, ſlides along the Way, and breaks forth into particular Streams in ſome places, which fall
with

with a great impetuofity and noife, and make a very pleafant found and fight.

We meet not here with thofe fine Caftles to be feen on the Banks of the Loire, which make Travellers call it the Country of Fairies. Here are on thefe Mountains only fome Shepherds Cottages, and fome few Hovels, and at that diftance, that you muft go a great way before you can find them; yet all thefe Natural Objects, though very melancholly ones, yet have fomething that is very taking in them. The Snows were fo high, that we had always twenty Men, who made way for us with Shovels. You will perhaps imagine this coft me very much; but here are fo well eftablifht Orders, and thofe fo well obferv'd, that the Inhabitants of a Village are oblig'd to meet Travellers, and be their Guides to the next; and no one being bound to give them any thing, the leaft Liberality therefore fatisfies them.

them. To this firſt Care there is added another, which is that of Ringing the Bells without ceaſing, to give notice to Travellers, where they may retreat in ſtormy Weather. They told me, there had not fall'n this forty Years ſo much Snow as we met with, there having been no Froſt for a great while in this Province.

Our Troop was ſo great that we might count ourſelves no ways inferiour to thoſe Famous Caravans which go to Mecha; for without reckoning my Train, and that of Don Fernand de Toledo, there joyn'd with us near St. Sebaſtian, three Knights, with their Attendants, who return'd from their Commanderſhips of St. James; there were two of this Order, and one of that of Alcantara: The firſt wear Red Croſſes, in form of an embroidered Sword, on their Shoulders; and he of Alcantara had a Green one. One of the two firſt is of Andalouſia, the other of Galicia, and the third of Catalonia; they

they are of good Families; he of Andaloufia calls himfelf, Don Efteve de Carvajal; he of Galicia, Don Sancho Sanniento; and the other of Catalonia, Don Frederic de Cardonne; they are Perfons of good Meine, and well acquainted with the World. I receiv'd all poffible Civilities from them, having much of the French Humour in them. They have travelled over the greateft Part of Europe; and this has rendred them fo Polite. We went to lye at Galareta; this is a Borough a little diftant from Mount Adrian, fituated in the little Province of Spain, I now mention'd, named Alava, which makes a Part of Biscaye; we had there but bad Entertainment. They reckon it eleven Leagues from thence to St. Sebaftian.

We had better Way from Galareta to Victoria, than we had before: The Country here yields much Corn and Grapes; and the Villages lie very thick together: We found here Cuftomtom-Houſe-Men, who made us pay both for the Cloaths and Money we carried with us: they were not very exacting with us, becauſe our Company was too large to be impoſed on. Don Fernand de Toledo had inform'd me over Night, that we were to travel near the Caſtle of Quebare, which was ſaid to be haunted with a Spirit, telling me a thouſand extravagant Stories, which were readily ſwallow'd by the Inhabitants of the Country, and which were ſo effectually believ'd by them, that no body would live there. I had a great deſire to ſee this place; for altho' I am naturally as fearful as another, yet am not afraid of Ghoſts; and if I were, our Company was ſo numerous, as would animate the greateſt Coward: we ſtruck off a little to the left, and came to the Borough of Quebara; the Maſter of the Inn where we entred, had the Keys of the Caſtle; he told us, in going along with us, 'That the Duende,'

ende,' which is to say the Spirit, 'could not endure Company; yet if we were a thousand together, he would, if he were minded, beat us all, in such a manner, as to leave us for dead.' I began to tremble; Don Fernand de Toledo, and Don Frederic de Cordonne, who gave me their Hands, perceiving my Fear, burst out into Laughter: I grew asham'd, and pretended to gain Courage; and so we entred the Castle, which might have past for a fine one, had it been kept in order: It had no Furniture, except an old Tapistry Hanging in a great Hall, which represented the Amours of Don Pedro the Cruel, and Donna Maria de Padilla: she is represented sitting like a Queen in the midst of other Ladies, and the King placing on her Head a Crown of Flowers: In another part she sate under the shade of a Wood, the King shewing her a Hawk on his Fist: And again, in another, she appears in a Warrier's Dress, and the King

King in Armour prefents her with a Sword; which makes me believe that fhe had been in fome Warlike Expedition with him. She was very ill reprefented; and Don Fernand told me, 'He had feen her Effigies elfewhere, by which fhe appeared to be the moft beautiful and moft cruel Woman of her time; and that the Figures in this Tapiftry refembled neither her nor the King: his Name, Cypher, and Arms were every-where on it.' We went up into a Tower, on the top of which was a Dungeon, and 'twas there where the Spirit inhabited; but without doubt he was abroad, for we neither faw nor heard him, or any of his Companions; and having feen fufficiently this great Building, we left it to purfue our Journey. In approaching Victoria, we paft over a moft delightful Plain, at the end of which ftands a Town fituated in this Province of Spain, I lately mention'd, call'd Alava; this is

the

the Capital Town of it, as well as the firſt of Caſtille: It is incloſed with two Walls, one of which is old, and the other new; beſides this, it has no other Fortifications. After I had refreſh'd myſelf a while here, 'twas propoſed to me to go to a Play; but in tarrying till it began, I had no ſmall Diverſion, in ſeeing come into the moſt ſpacious place of the Town, four Companies of young Men, preceded by Drums and Trumpets: they marched ſeveral times round, and in fine, immediately began the Fight with Snow-balls, which they threw at one another with ſuch Fierceneſs, that they were all very well pelted in the end: they were above two hundred who fought this Battle. To tell you of thoſe who fell, or recovered their Feet again, and the Shouts and Acclamations of the People, will be needleſs; and I was obliged to leave them thus engaged, to go to the place where the Play was to be repreſented.

When

When I entred into the Room, the People set forth an hollowing, Mira, mira! which is to say, Look, look! The Decoration of the Theatre was not over Magnificent; it was rais'd on Barrels, and ill-rang'd Planks; the Windows of the Room were open, for they used no Candles or Flambeaux; whence you can easily imagine this much takes away from the Beauty of the Sight. They acted the Life of St. Anthony; and when the Players said any thing which pleas'd the Company, all the People cried out, Victoria, Victoria; I was informed this was the Custom of the Country. I observ'd the Devil was no other ways clad than the rest, having only a pair of Stockings of a Flame colour, and a pair of Horns to distinguish him. This Comedy consisted only of three Acts, and they are all no more: at the end of each serious Act, another began of Farce and Pleasantry, wherein appear'd him they called El Gracioso, which

which is to say, the Buffoon, who, among much insipid Stuff, says sometimes something that is less nauseous: The Interludes were mixt with Dances, to the sound of the Harps and Guitars: The Actors had Castagnets, and a little Hat on their Heads, without which they never Dance, and then 'tis a Saraband; they seem not to walk, they slip along so lightly. Their manner is wholly different from ours: they move too much their Arms, and often pass their Hands on their Hats and Face, and that with no ill Grace; they play admirably well on the Castagnets.

As to the rest, (Dear Cousin) I would not have you think these Actors, for being in a little City, do much differ from those of Madrid. I was told that those of the King are a little better; but, in a word, both act what they call Las Comedias Famosas, which is to say, The finest and most famous Comedies; which in truth are
very

very ridiculous: For Example, when St. Anthony faid his Confiteor, which he did often enough, all the Spectators fell down on their Knees, and gave themfelves fuch rude Mea Culpa's as was enough to beat the breath out of their Bodies.

Here would be a proper place to fpeak of their Habits; but you had better excufe me till I come to Madrid, left I tire you with Repetitions: Yet I muft tell you, that all the Ladies I faw in this Company, had a prodigious quantity of Red, which begins juft under the Eye, and paffes from the Chin to the Ears, and Shoulders, to their very Hands; fo that I never faw any Radifhes of a finer Colour.

The Lady Governnefs of the Town drew near to me; fhe juft toucht my Cloaths, and haftily drew back her Hand as if fhe had burnt her Fingers. I bid her in Spanifh not to be afraid: She at length familiariz'd herfelf, and told me, ' 'Twas not through fear of any

any thing else but of displeasing me: that 'twas no new thing to her to see French Ladies: and that if she might, she would gladly dress herself after their Fashion.' She ordered Chocolate to be brought her, with which she presented me; which is far better here than in France. The Play being ended, I took my Leave of her, having thanked her for her Civilities.

The next Morning, as I entred the Church to hear Mass, I espied an Hermit, who had the Air of a Person of Quality, and yet begg'd an Alms of me, with such great Humility, that I was greatly surpriz'd at it: Don Fernand having notice of it, drew near, and said to me, 'The Person whom you behold, Madam, is of an Illustrious Family, and of great Merit, but his Fortune very Unhappy.'

'You raise in me,' said I to him, 'a great Curiosity to know more; and therefore I must beg your Favour to satisfie it.' 'You may command any thing

thing of me,' replied he, 'Madam; but I am not so thoroughly inform'd of his Adventures, to undertake the relating them to you; and I believe 'twere better I engage him into a Recital of them himself.' He left me, and went immediately to Embrace him, with the greatest Civilities and Tenderness: Don Frederic de Cardonne, and Don Esteve de Carvajal, had already accosted him, as their old Acquaintance; and when Don Fernand had joyn'd them, they all earnestly intreated him to come with them when Mass was over. He as earnestly excused himself; but being told, I was a Stranger, and much importuned, that I might learn from himself, what had oblig'd him to turn Hermit; he at length consented, on condition I would permit him to bring one of his Friends, who was perfectly knowing in what related to him: 'Do us Justice,' continued he, 'and judge whether 'tis fit for me to relate such Particularities in this

this Habit I wear.' They found he had Reason, and pray'd him to bring his Friend, which he did a while after I was at my Lodgings: He presented a very fine Cavalier to me; and taking leave of us very civilly, he told him, 'He should be oblig'd to him, if he would satisfie the Curiosity which Don Fernand de Toledo had giv'n me, of knowing the Spring of his Misfortunes.' This Gentleman took place by me, and began in these Terms:

'I think myself very Happy, Madam, that my Friend has chosen me to satisfie the Desire you have of knowing his Adventures; but I fear I shall not acquit myself so well as I would: The Person whose History you wou'd learn, has been one of the finest Gentlemen in the World; it would be hard to make a Judgment of him now; he is buried, as it were in his Hermit's Habit. He was an exceeding graceful Person, well shaped, of an excellent Meine, and Noble Air: And in fine,
had

had all the Accomplishments, both Natural and Acquired, of a Person of Quality, being liberal, witty and brave. He was born at Cagliari, Capital of the Isle of Sardogne, one of the most illustrious and richest Families of all that Country.

'He was brought up with one of his Cousin-Germans; and the sympathy which was found in their Humours, and Inclinations, was so great, that they were more strictly united by Friendship than Blood: they had no Secret from each other. And when the Marquifs Barbaran was married (which was his Cousin's Name,) their Friendship continued in the same force.

'He married one of the finest Women in the World, and the most Accomphisht; she was then not above Fourteen: She was Heiress to a very Noble Estate and Family. The Marquess every day discovered new Charms in the Wit and Person of his Wife, which like-

likewise increased every day his Passion. He speaks without ceasing, of his Happiness, to Don Lewis de Barbaran; which is the Name, Madam, of my Friend; and when any Affairs oblig'd the Marquess to leave her, he conjured him to stay with the Marchioness, thereby to lessen the Trouble of his Absence. But alas! how hard is it when one is at an Age uncapable of serious Reflections, to see continually so fine a Woman, so young and aimable; and to see her with Indifference! Don Lewis was already desperately in Love with the Marchioness, and thought then 'twas only for her Husband's sake: Whilst he was in this Mistake, she fell dangerously sick; at which he grew so dreadful melancholly, that he then knew, but too late, this was caus'd by a Passion which would prove the greatest Misfortune of his whole Life. Finding himself then in this condition, and having not strength to resist it, he resolv'd folv'd to ufe the utmoft Extremity, and to fly and avoid a place where he was in danger of dying with Love, or breaking through the Bonds of Friendfhip. The moft cruel Death wou'd have feem gentler than the Execution of this Defign: When the Marchionefs beginning to grow better, he went to her to bid her Adieu, and fee her no more.

'He found her bufied in choofing among feveral Stones of great price, thofe which were the fineft, which fhe intended to have fet in a Ring, Don Lewis was fcarce entred the Chamber, but fhe defired him, with that Air of Familiarity ufual among Relations, to go and fetch her other Stones which fhe moreover had in her Cabinet. He ran thither, and by an unexpected good hap, found among what he lookt for, the Picture enamell'd of the Marchionefs, in little, fet with Diamonds, and incircled with a Lock of her Hair; it was fo like,
that

that he had not the power to withstand the defire he had of ftealing it: "I am going to leave her," faid he, "I fhall fee her no more; I facrifice all my quiet to her Husband: Alas! is not this enough? And may I not without a Crime, fearch in my Pain a Confolation fo innocent as this." He kift feveral times this Picture; he put it under his Arm, he carefully hid it, and returning towards her with thefe Stones, he tremblingly told her the Refolution he had taken of Travelling. She appear'd much amazed at it, and chang'd her colour. He lookt on her at this moment; he had the pleafure of perceiving it; and their Eyes being of Intelligence, fpake more than their Words: "Alas! What can oblige you, Don Lewis," faid fhe to him, "to leave us? Your Coufin loves you fo tenderly; I efteem you; we are never pleas'd without you; he cannot live from you: Have you not already travelled? You have without doubt

doubt some other Reason for your Departure, but at least do not hide it from me." Don Lewis, pierc'd through with sorrow, could not forbear uttering a deep Sigh, and taking one of the delicate Hands of the Charming Person, on which he fixt his Mouth, "Ah, Madam, What do you ask me?" said he to her, "What would you have me say to you? And indeed, What can I say to you, in the Condition I am in?" The Violence he used, to conceal his Sentiments, caus'd him such a great Weakness, that he fell half dead at her Feet. She remained troubled and confused at this sight: She oblig'd him to sit down by her; she dared not lift up her Eyes to look on him; but she let him see Tears, which she could not forbear shedding, nor resolve to conceal from him.

'Scarcely were they come to themselves, when the Marquess entred into the Chamber. He came to embrace Don

Don Lewis with all the Teſtimonies of a perfect Friendſhip, and he was in the greateſt trouble, when he underſtood he parted for Naples. He omitted no Arguments to perſwade him from it, preſt his ſtay with the greateſt Earneſtneſs, but all in vain. He there immediately took his leave of the Marchioneſs, and ſaw her no more. The Marqueſs went out with him, he left him not till the moment of his Departure. This was an Augmentation of Don Lewis's Sorrow; he would have willingly remained alone to have an intire Liberty of afflicting himſelf.

'The Marchioneſs was fenſibly afflicted at this Separation: She had perceived he loved her, before he had known thus much himſelf; and ſhe had found in him ſuch ſingular Merit, that for her part too ſhe had loved him without knowing it; but ſhe found this to her Coſt after his Departure: Recovering but lately from a danger-

dangerous Sickneſs, of which ſhe was not perfectly cured, this unhappy Accident made her fall into a languiſhing Indiſpoſition, as ſoon rendred her quite another body; her Duty, her Reaſon, her Vertue equally perſecuted her: She was greatly ſenſible of her Husband's Reſpects to her, and ſhe could not ſuffer but with great Sorrow, that another ſhould take up her Thoughts, and have ſo great a place in her Affections. She dared not any more mention the Name of Don Lewis; ſhe never made any Enquiries after him; ſhe made it an indiſpenſable Duty to forget him: This Violence which ſhe uſed on herſelf, was like a continual Martyrdom; ſhe made one of her Women, In whom ſhe moſt confided, the Repoſitory of this Secret: "Am I not very unhappy?" ſaid ſhe, "I muſt wiſh never again to ſee a Man, towards whom it is impoſſible for me to be in a ſtate of Indifference; his Perſon is always before

fore mine Eyes; nay, I think sometimes I see him in the Person of my Husband; the Resemblance which is between them, serves only to nourish my Affection towards him. Alas! Mariana, I must die, to expiate this Crime, although it be an involuntary one; I have only this means to get rid of a Passion of which I cannot hitherto be Mistress: Alas, what have I not done to stifle it, this Passion which yet is dear to me." She accompany'd these Words with a thousand Sighs: She melted into Tears; and though this Woman had had a great deal of Wit and Affection to her Mistress, yet she could say nothing to her could yield her any Comfort.

'The Marquess in the mean time, every day reproacht his Wife with her Indifferency to Don Lewis: "I cannot suffer," said he to her, "that you should think so little on the Man I love above all the World, and who had so much Complaisance and Friendship

ſhip for you: I muſt needs ſay, this is a kind of Hardneſs, which would make one judge untowardly of the Tenderneſs of your Heart: At leaſt, you muſt grant, Madam, that he was ſcarcely gone, but you forgot him." "What good would my remembring him do him?" ſaid the Marchioneſs with a languiſhing Air, "Do not you ſee he avoids us? Would he not have been ſtill with us, if he had any real Kindneſs for us? Believe me, my Lord, he deſerves a little that we ſhould forſake him in our turn." Whatever ſhe could ſay, repel'd not the Marqueſs; he ſtill importun'd her to write to Don Lewis to Return. One Day among the reſt, ſhe was gotten into his Cloſet to ſpeak to him about ſome Affairs; ſhe found him buſied in reading a Letter of D. Lewis, which he lately receiv'd.

'She would have retir'd; but he took this opportunity to oblige her to do what he would have her; he told her

her very ſeriouſly, "That he could no longer bear the Abſence of his Couſin; that he was reſolv'd to go find him; that 'twas already two Years ſince he had been gone, without intimating any deſire of returning to his Friends and Country; that he was perſwaded he would yield a greater Deference to her Requeſts than his; that he conjured her to write to him: And that in fine, ſhe might chuſe either to give him this Satisfaction, or be content to ſee him part for Naples, where Don Lewis was to make ſome ſtay." She remain'd ſurpriz'd, and perplext at this Propoſal; but knowing he expected with great Impatience her Determination, "What would you have me ſay to him, my Lord?" ſaid ſhe to him with a ſorrowful Countenance, "Dictate this Letter to me, I will write it; I can do no more; and I believe this is more than I ought." The Marqueſs, tranſported with Joy, moſt affectionately embrac'd her; he thank'd

her

her for her Compliance, and made her write thefe Words:

"IF you have any Kindnefs for us, defer not your Return; I have very urgent Reafons to defire it. I am not a little concern'd that you fhew fuch Indifference towards us, which is an unqueftionable Indication that you take no Delight in our Company. Return, Don Lewis, I earneftly wifh it; I intreat you: And if it were fit for me to ufe more urgent Terms, I would fay, perhaps, I Command you to do it."

'The Marquefs made a fingle Pacquet of this fatal Letter, to the end Don Lewis might not think 'twas by his Order the Marchionefs had wrote it; and having fent it to the Currier, he expected the Succefs with extraordinary Impatience. What became of this Lover at the fight of fo dear and unexpected an Order! Although he he had remarkt Dispositions of Tenderness in the Countenance of this fair Person, yet he dared not promise himself she could desire his Return; his Reason revolted against his Joy: "How Unhappy a Wretch am I?" said he, "I Adore the most Aimable of all Women, and yet I dare not offer to please her! she has a Kindness for me, yet Honour and Friendship with-hold me from making the least Advantage of it. What shall I do then, O Heavens! What shall I do! I flatter'd my self, that Absence would Cure me: Alas! this is a Remedy which I have fruitlesly tried; I have never cast mine Eyes on her Picture, but have found myself more in Love, and more Miserable than when I saw her every day. I must obey her, she commands my Return; she desires to see me, and she cannot be ignorant of my Passion: When I took my Leave of her, my Eyes declared to her the Secret of my Heart: And when I call to mind what I faw in hers, all my Reflections then are to no purpofe; for I refolve rather to die at her Feet, than to live remote from her."

'He parted without any delay, and without taking leave of his Friends. He left a Gentleman to Excufe him towards them, and to order his Affairs. He was in fuch great hafte to fee the Marchionefs, that he ufed fuch Diligence to be with her, that no body but he could have done: In arriving at Cagliary, Capital of Sardagne, he underftood that the Marquefs and his Wife were at a ftately Country-houfe, where the Vice-Roy was gone to give them a Vifit, with all his Court. He learnt moreover, that the Marquefs de Barbaran prepared for him a great Feaft, where there were to be held Jufts or Turnaments, after the Ancient Manner of the Mores: He was the Defendant, and was to maintain, "That a Husband beloved, is Happier than a Lover."

'Several

'Several Gentlemen that were not of this Opinion, were preparing themſelves to go and diſpute the Prize, which the Marchioneſs, at the Vice-Queen's Intreaty, was to give to the Conquerour; 'Twas a Scarf embroidered with her own Hands, wrought with Cyphers: No one was to appear but maskt and diſguiſed, to the end all might be freer and more gallant.

'Don Lewis had a ſecret Deſpight, in comprehending the Marqueſs ſo well ſatisfied: "He is belov'd," ſaid he, "I cannot but look on him as my Rival, and as an Happy Rival; but we muſt endeavour to diſturb his Happineſs, in triumphing over his vain Glory." Having formed this Deſign, he would not appear in Town; he cauſ'd to be made a Suit of ſtrip'd Green Satin, embroidered with Gold, and all his Liveries were of the ſame Colour, to denote his new Hopes.

'When he entred into the Lisſts, everybody had their Eyes on him; his
Mag-

Magnificence and his Air gave Emulation to the Cavaliers, and great Curiosity to the Ladies. The Marchioness felt a secret Emotion, of which she could not discover the Cause: He was placed very near the Balcony, where she sate with the Vice-Queen; but there was no Lady there which did not lose all her Lustre near that of the Marchioness; her youthful Air, which exceeded not eighteen Years, her lovely white and red Cheeks, her Eyes so sweet and graceful, her Scarlet and little Mouth, agreeable Smiles, and her Shape, which surpast the Fairest, made her the Admiration of all the World.

'Don Lewis was so ravish'd in seeing her so charming, and to observe yet in her Countenance a languishing sorrowful Air, that he flattered himself to have therein a part; and this was the first Moment wherein he thought himself Happy. When his turn came, he ran against the Marquess, and smote him

him so dexterously, that he got the Advantage all along of him: so that in a word, he gain'd the Prize with a general Applause, and with every one's good-liking. He threw himself at the Marchioness's Feet, to receive it at her Hands; he altered the Tone of his Voice, and speaking to her with his Mask on, low enough not to be heard but only by her: "Divine Person," said he to her, "be pleas'd to observe what Fortune decides in favour of Lovers." He dar'd not say more to her; and without knowing him, she gave him the Prize, with this natural Grace with which all her Actions were accompanied.

'He suddenly withdrew himself, for fear of being known; for this might have been an occasion of Quarrel between the Marquess and him; and without doubt he would not have easily pardon'd the Victory he obtain'd over him. This oblig'd him to keep himself still conceal'd for some Days.

Days. The Vice-Roy and his Lady return'd to Cagliari, and the Marquefs and Marchionefs accompanied them thither, with the whole Court.

'Don Lewis then fhew'd himfelf; he pretended he juft then arriv'd, and made as if he knew not what had paft in the Field. The Marquefs de Barbaran was tranfported with Joy in feeing him; and Abfence had not at all altered the Affection he had for this dear Relation. He had no difficult task to find a favourable moment wherein to entertain his aimable Marchionefs; he had as much liberty in their Lodgings as in his own; and you may well judge, Madam, that he forgot not to mention the Prize he had receiv'd from her fair Hands. "How wretched am I," faid he to her, "that you did not know me? Alas, Madam, I flattered myfelf, that by fome fecret Pre-fentiments you would learn, that no one but I could fuftain with fuch Paffion the Caufe of
Lovers

Lovers againſt Husbands." "No my Lord," ſaid ſhe to him, with an Angry and Diſdainful Air, to take away all Hope from him, "I could never have imagin'd that you could have been Patron of ſo foul a Cauſe; and I could not have believ'd you could have taken ſuch ſtrong Engagements at Naples, that you ſhould come as far as Sardagne to Triumph over a Friend who maintain'd my Intereſts as well as his own." "I ſhall die with Regret, Madam," ſaid Don Lewis, "if I have diſpleas'd you in what I have done; and were you more favourably diſpoſed, and I might dare to make you my Confident, it would be no hard matter for me to perſuade you, that it is not at Naples I have left the Object of my Vows."

'The Marchioneſs apprehending leſt he ſhould ſpeak more than ſhe was willing to hear, and appear livelily toucht with the Reproach ſhe made him, ſhe put on a more pleaſing Countenance,

tenance, and turning the Converſation into a Tone of Raillery, anſwer'd him, "He took too ſeriouſly what ſhe had ſaid to him." He dared not make uſe of this occaſion to declare his Love to her; for though he lov'd her above all things, yet he reſpected her no leſs.

'When he had left her, he began to blame himſelf for his Fearfulneſs: "Shall I," ſaid he, "always ſuffer without ſeeking any Remedy!" It was ſome time before he could meet with a favourable occaſion, becauſe the Marchioneſs ſtudiouſly avoided him; but being come one Night where ſhe was, he found her alone in an inward room, lying on a Bed in a moſt lovely manner, and moſt becoming Undreſs, her Hair being faſtned with Knots of Diamonds, hung careleſly about her Breaſts: The Trouble ſhe felt in ſeeing Don Lewis, appear'd on her Countenance, and rendred her yet more lovely: He drew near her with an Awful and Reſpectful Air, fell down on his Knees

Knees by her; he lookt on her for some time, not daring to speak, but becoming a little more bold, "If you consider, Madam," said he to her, "the piteous Condition whereto you have reduced me, you will easily comprehend that it is no longer in my power to keep Silence: I could not avoid such inevitable Stroaks as you have given me; I have adored you as soon as I saw you: I have endeavour'd to Cure myself in flying from you; I have offered the greatest Violence to myself, in endeavouring to master my Passion. You have recall'd me, Madam, from my Voluntary Exile, and I die a thousand times a Day, uncertain of my Destiny: If you be Cruel enough to refuse me your Pity, suffer at least, that having made known to you my Passion, I may die with Grief at your Feet." The Marchioness was some time without resolving to answer him; but at length, gaining Assurance, "I acknowledge," said she, "Don Lewis, that

that I am not wholly ignorant of one part of your Sentiments, but I was willing to perſwade myſelf 'twas the Effects of an Innocent Affection: Make me not a Partner of your Crime; you commit one, when you betray the Friendſhip due to my Husband: But, alas, you will pay but too dearly for this; for I know that Duty forbids you to Love me; and in my Reſpect, it does not only forbid me to love you, but to fly from you: I will do it, Don Lewis, I will avoid you; and I do not know, whether I ought not to Hate you: But, alas, it ſeems impoſſible to me to do it." "What do you then, Madam," anſwer'd he, interrupting her, being full of Grief and Deſpair, "when you pronounce the Sentence of my Death? You cannot Hate me, ſay you; Do you not Hate me, and do you not do me all the Miſchief you are able, when you reſolve to avoid me? Make an end, Madam, make an end, leave not your
Ven-

Vengeance imperfect; sacrifice me to your Duty, and your Husband; for my Life cannot but be odious, if you take from me the Hopes of pleasing you." She lookt on him at this instant with Eyes full of Languishment: "Don Lewis," said she to him, "you reproach me with what I would deserve." In ending these words, she arose, fearing greatly, lest her Affection should triumph over her Reason; and notwithstanding his endeavours to with-hold her, she past into a Chamber where her Women were.

'She thought she had gained much on herself in forcing her way out of this Conversation without answering so favourably as her Heart could have wisht; but Love is a Seducer, which must not be in any sort hearkened to, if one will not be totally overcome by him. From that day Don Lewis began to think himself Happy, though he wanted many things to compleat his Felicity. The Marchioness, in effect,

fect, had a Principle of Vertue which oppofed itfelf always with Succefs to the defires of her Lover.

'He had no longer thofe Scruples of Friendfhip for the Marquefs de Barbaran which had fo greatly difturbed his Mind; Love had perfectly banifht Friendfhip; nay, he even fecretly hated him.

'In fine, Don Lewis flattering himfelf, that perhaps he might find a favourable moment to affect the Marchionefs's Heart with fome Pity; he carefully fought it; and to find it, one day when 'twas very hot, knowing that the Marchionefs was wont to retire to Repofe herfelf after Dinner, as it is cuftomary in that Country, he came to her, doubting not but every body was afleep in the Houfe.

'She was in a Ground-Room which lookt into the Garden; all was faft and fhut clofe, fave a little Window, whereby he faw on her Bed this charming Creature: She was in a profound

found Sleep, half undreſt; he had the time to diſcover ſuch Beauties as ſtill augmented the force of his Paſſion. He approacht ſo ſoftly to her, that ſhe did not awake: It was already ſome moments that he had lookt on her with all the Tranſports of a Man amazed, when ſeeing her naked Breaſts, he could not forbear kiſſing them. She aroſe on a ſudden; ſhe had not her Eyes open; the Chamber was dark, and ſhe could never have believ'd Don Lewis could have been ſo bold. I have already told you, Madam, that he reſembled the Marqueſs de Barbaran; She did not doubt then but it was he, and calling him ſeveral times, "her dear Marqueſs and Husband," ſhe tenderly embrac'd him. He well knew his Error; whatever Pleaſure it procured him, he could have wiſhed to have ow'd this only to his Miſtreſs's Favours. But, O Heavens, how unfortunately it hapned! The Marqueſs came in this dangerous

ous moment; and 'twas not without the greateſt fury he ſaw the Liberty Don Lewis took with his Wife. At the noiſe he had made in entring, ſhe had turn'd her Eyes towards the Door, and ſeeing her Husband enter, whom ſhe thought ſhe had already in her arms, it is impoſſible to repreſent her Affliction and Aſtoniſhment.

'Don Lewis amaz'd at this Accident, flatter'd himſelf, that perhaps he was not known: He paſt immediately into the Gallery, and finding a Window was opened into the Garden, he threw himſelf out of it, and immediately paſt through a Back-door. The Marqueſs purſued him, without being able to overtake him: In returning the ſame way he came, he unhappily found the Marchioneſs's Picture, which Don Lewis had dropt as he ran; he immediately made moſt cruel Reflections hereupon: This Picture of his Wife, which Don Lewis had let fall, and the ſight of her embracing him,
all

all this made him no longer doubt of his Wives Falshood: "I am betray'd," Cry'd he, "by her whom I loved dearer than my own Life: Was there ever a more Unhappy Man in the World?" In ending these Words, he returned to his Wives Chamber. She immediately threw herself at his Feet, and melting into Tears, would have justify'd herself, and make known to him her Innocency; but the Spirit of Jealousie had so fully possest him, that he violently represt her: He harkned only to the Transports of his Rage and Despair, and turning away his Eyes, that he might not see so lovely an Object, he had the Barbarity to strike his Dagger into the Breast of the most Beautiful and most Vertuous Woman in the World. She offered herself to be slaughtered as an innocent Sacrifice, and her Soul issued out in a stream of Blood.

"O God," cryed I, "O Imprudent Don Lewis! Why did you leave this Charm-

Charming Lady to the Fury of an Amorous Husband, tranſported with Jealouſie! You might have ſnatch'd her out of his cruel Hands." "Alas, Madam," replied this Gentleman, "he know not what he did; for what would he have done at another time to have prevented ſuch a Misfortune."

'As ſoon as the unfortunate Marchioneſs had rendred her laſt Breath, her cruel Executioner ſhut her Apartment, took all the Money and Jewels he had, mounted on Horſe-back, and fled with all the ſpeed he could. Don Lewis reſtleſs, and more Amorous than ever, returned thither in the Evening, notwithſtanding whatever might befal him: He was ſurpriz'd when he was told the Marchioneſs was ſtill aſleep; he immediately went into the Garden, and entred into the Gallery, through the ſame Window which he had found open, and from thence came into the Chamber: 'Twas ſo dark, that he was fain to walk warily;

warily; when he felt something which had like to have made him fall, he stooped down, and found it was a dead Body; he uttered a great Shriek, and doubting not but it was that of his dear Mistress, he sunk down with Grief: Some of the Marchioness's Women walking under the Windows of her Apartment, heard Don Lewis's Crys; they easily got up through the same Window, and entred the Room. What a sad Spectacle, what a lamentable sight was this? I cannot find Words to denote to you the Horror of this Spectacle. Don Lewis was no sooner come to himself, by the force of Remedies, but his Grief, Rage and Despair, broke out with such Violence, that it was impossible to calm him; and I am perswaded he had not outlived her whose loss he occasioned, if the desire of Vengeance had not re-animated him.

'He parted like one furious in search of the Marquess de Barbaran; He fought

fought him every-where without hearing any news of him; He ran over Italy, traverſt Germany, came into Flanders, and paſt into France. He was told that the Marqueſs was at Valentia in Spain; he came there, and met not with him. In fine, three Years being paſt, without finding the means of ſacrificing his Enemy to his Miſtreſs's Ghoſt, Divine Grace, which is irreſiſtible, and particularly on great Souls, toucht his ſo efficatiouſly, that he immediately changed his Deſire of Revenge into ſerious Deſires of leaving the World, and minding only the fitting himſelf for another Life.

'Being fill'd with this Spirit he return'd into Sardagnia: He ſold all his Eſtate, which he diſtributed among ſome of his Friends, who with great Merit were yet very poor; and by this means became ſo poor himſelf, that he reduced himſelf to the begging of Alms.

'He had heretofore ſeen, in going
to

to Madrid, a place very fit to make an Hermitage, (it is towards Mount Dragon;) this Mountain is almoſt inacceſſible, and you cannot paſs to it but through an Overture, which is in the midſt of a great Rock; it is ſtopt up when the Snow falls, and the Hermitage lies buried more than ſix Months under it. Don Lewis made one be built here, where he was wont to paſs whole Years without ſeeing any one. He made ſuch Proviſions as were neceſſary, having good Books, and thus remain'd in this diſmal Solitude; but this Year his Friends forced him hither, by reaſon of a great Sickneſs, which had like to have coſt him his Life. It is four Years ſince he has led this Holy Spiritual Life, and ſo different from that to which he was born, that it is with great trouble he ſees any of his Acquaintance.

'As to the Marqueſs de Barbaran, he has wholly left the Iſle of Sardagnia,

dagnia, where he has not the Liberty to return. I am inform'd he is married again at Anvers, to a Widow of a Spaniard named Fonceca.

'And it is he himſelf that has related to one of my Friends the Particularities of his Crime; and he is ſo furiouſly tortured with the remembrance of it, that he imagines he continually ſees his Wife dying, and reproaching him with his Fury and Jealouſie. In a word, he has contracted ſuch a deep Malancholly, that his Death is thought by every one to be near, or at the leaſt, the loſs of his Sences.'

The Gentleman here was ſilent; and I not being able to forbear weeping at ſo Tragical a Relation, Don Fernand de Toledo, who had obſerv'd it, and would not take notice of it, for fear of interrupting the Relation, rally'd me about my Tenderneſs, telling me how well he was pleaſed to find me ſo Compaſſionate, and that I ſhould not be long before I met with Objects

jects fit to exercise it on. I did not so much mind the returning an answer to him, as the Thanking this Gentleman, who was pleas'd to entertain me with the Recital of so extraordinary an Adventure: I intreated him to make my Compliments to Don Lewis, and to give him from me two Pistols, seeing he lived on Alms. Don Fernand, and each of the Cavaliers, gave as much: 'Here is,' said the Gentleman to us, 'wherewith to enrich the Poor of Victoria; for Don Lewis appropriates not such great Charities as these to himself.' We told him, he was the Master, and might dispose of the Money as he pleased. But to return to my Adventures:

Although I had a Pasport from the King of Spain, the best specified, and most general, as is possible, yet I was oblig'd to take a Billet from the Toll-House; for without this Precaution, all my Cloaths had been confiscated: 'To what purpose then is my Pasport?'

port?' said I to them. 'To none at all,' replied they. The Surveyors and Officers of the Customs would not so much as cast their Eyes on it; they told me, The King must come and assure them, that this Order was from him. It is to no purpose for any one to alledge his being a Stranger, and ignorant of the Usages of the Country: For they drily answer, 'That the Stranger's Ignorance makes the Spaniard's Profit.' The ill Weather has kept me here two Days, during which I saw the Governness, and the Play. The principal Place of this Town is adorn'd with a very fair Fountain standing in the midst: it is incircled with the Town-House, the Prison, two Convents, and several well-built Houses: Here is a New Town and an Old one; every body forsakes this latter to dwell in the other. Here are very rich Merchants; their chief Trade is at St. Sebastian or Bilbo; they send great store of Iron to Grenada, Estremadour,

madour, Galicia, and other Parts of the Kingdom. I obferv'd, that the great Streets are fet with fine Trees, which are watered with Streams running by them. From Mount St. Adrian hither, it is feven Leagues. In fine, I am juft fetting out, and muft end this long Letter; it is late, and I have fpoke to you fo much of what I have feen, that I have faid nothing of my Affections to you: Believe me, however, Dear Coufin, that I am, and ever fhall be

Yours.

From Victoria,
   Feb. 24, 1673.

Letter III

MY Letters are so long, that it is hard to believe when I finish them, that I have any thing else more to tell you; yet, my dear Cousin, I never close any, but there remains still sufficient for another: When I were onely to speak to you of my Friendship, this would be an inexhaustible Subject; you may make some Judgment of it from the Pleasure I find in obeying your Commands. You are desirous to know all the Particulars of my Voyage, I will therefore go on to relate them:

I set out very late from Victoria, by reason of my stay at the Governness's, whom I before mention'd; and we went to lie at Miranda; the Country is very pleasant as far as Avigny; we
came

A Town of Central Spain

LETTER III.

Mr. ———, you are so long that is in believing when I tell them, that I have any thing else more to tell you, that my dear Cousin, I have that ——, but then a reason sufficient ——

A Tour of Part of Spain

—————— is an innumerable —————— make such long —————— the Pleasure I had in —————— ——————. You are —————— to know all the Particulars of my Voyage, I shall therefore go on to relate them:

I set out very late from Valencia, by reason of my —— of the Greyhounds, where I had —— a Passage, and we went to lie at —————— the Country is very pleasant —— as far as Avigny; we came

came afterwards by a difficult Way to the Banks of the River Urola, whose Noise is the greater, in that 'tis full of Rocks, on which the Water dashes, beats up, and falls down, and forms natural Cascades in several places: We continu'd to ascend the high Mountains of the Pyrenees, where we ran a thousand several Dangers: we saw the ancient Ruines of an old Castle, where Ghosts and Spirits have their Apartments, as well as in that of Quebara, it is near Gargason; and being to stop there to shew my Passport, because here certain Customs are paid to the King, I learnt from the Alcade of the Borough, who drew near my Litter to talk with me, that it is the common Report of the Country, That there were formerly a King and a Queen here, who had so fine and beautiful a Woman to their Daughter, that she was rather taken for a Goddess than a Mortal Creature: she was call'd Mira; and it is from her Name came

came the Mira of the Spaniards, which is to ſay, 'Look you'; for as ſoon as ever ſhe appear'd, all the People attentively beheld her, and cried out, 'Mira, Mira'; and here's the Etymology of a Word drawn far enough. This Princeſs was never ſeen by any Body who became not deſperately in love with her; but her Diſdainfulneſs and Indifference made all her Lovers pine away: The famous Baſiliſk never kill'd ſo many People as the Beautiful and Dreadful Mira; ſhe thus depopulated her Father's Kingdom, and all the Countries thereabouts were full of the deceaſed and dying Lovers. After they had in vain Addreſt themſelves to her, they laſtly applied themſelves to Heaven, to demand Vengeance on her Cruelty: The Gods at length grew Angry, and the Goddeſſes were not much behind them in the Exerciſe of this Paſſion: ſo that to puniſh her, the Scourges of Heaven finiſh'd the Deſtruction of

her

her Father's Kingdom: In this general Calamity he confulted the Oracle, which told him, 'That all thefe Miferies would not have an end, till Maria had expiated the Mischiefs which her Eyes had done; and that fhe muft be gone: That Deftiny would conduct her to th' place where fhe was to lofe her repofe and liberty.' The Princefs obey'd, believing it impofible for her to be touch'd with Tendernefs: She carried only her Nurfe with her; fhe was clad like a fimple Shepherdefs, left fhe fhould be taken notice of, whether at Sea or Land. She ran over a great Part of the World, committing every day two or three Dozen of Murthers; for her Beauty was not diminifht by the Fatigue of her Travels: She arriv'd at length near this old Caftle, which belong'd to a young Count, call'd Nios, endowed with a thoufand Perfections, but extream Proud and Referv'd: he pfent his time in the Woods; as foon as

ever

ever he perceiv'd a Woman, he fled from her, and of all Things he faw in the World, fhe was his greateft Averfion. The beautiful Mira was refting herfelf one day under the fhade of fome Trees, when Nios paft by, cloathed with a Lion's Skin, a Bow at his Girdle, and a Mace on his Shoulder; his Hair was all clotted together, and his Face be-fmear'd like a Chimney-Sweeper's, (this Circumstance is obfervable) yet the Princefs thought him the moft handfome Man in the World; fhe ran after him as if fhe had been mad; and he ran from her as if he had been in the fame condition: fhe loft the fight of him; fhe knew not where to find him: fhe is now in the greateft Sorrow, weeping Day and Night with her Nurfe. Nios return'd to the Chafe; fhe faw him again, and would have follow'd him: as foon as he perceiv'd her, he did as at firft, and Mira betook herfelf again to her Lamentations; but her Paffion giving her new ftrength,

strength, she out-ran him, stopt him, taking hold of his Locks, intreating him to look on her, thinking this was enough to engage him: He cast his Eyes on her with as much Indifference as if she had been an ordinary Person. Never Woman was more surpriz'd; she would not leave him; she came maugre him to his Castle: where, as soon as she had entred, he there left her, and was no more seen. The poor Mira, being not to be comforted, died with Grief: And from that time you hear deep Sighs and Groans which come from the Castle of Nios. The young Wenches of the Country are used to go there, and carry her little Presents of Fruits and Milk, which they set down at the Mouth of a Cave, where no body dare enter: they said, this was to comfort her; but this has been abolisht as superstitious. And though I believed not a word of whatever was told me at Garganson, in relation to Mira and
Nios,

Nios, yet I was pleas'd in the Recital of this Story, of which I omit a thousand Particulars, for fear of tiring you by its length. My Waiting-woman was so affected with this Relation, that she was for having us return back again, to set at the Mouth of the Cave some red Partridges, which my People had bought: she imagin'd the Princess's Ghost would be mightily comforted in receiving this Testimony of our good Will; but for my part, I thought I should be more content than her, in having those Partridges for my Supper. We past the River of Urola, on a great Stone-Bridge, and having went over another, with difficulty enough, by reason of the melted Snow, we arriv'd at Miranda d' Ebro; this is a great Village, or a little Town: here is a large place adorn'd with a Fountain; the River Ebro, which is one of the most considerable of Spain, traverses it: You see on the Top of a Mountain the Castle, with several Towers;

Towers; it appears to be of some strength; and there issues out so great a Stream from a Rock on which it is built, that it turns several Mills: I could not observe any thing else worth writing to you.

The three Knights I spake of to you, were arriv'd before me, and giv'n all requisite Orders for Supper; so we eat together: And tho' the Night appear'd well advanced, because the Days are short in this Season, yet 'twas not late; so that these Gentlemen, who shew'd me great Respect and Civility, askt me, How I would pass the time? I proposed to them the playing at Ombre, and that I would go Halves with Don Fernand de Toledo. They accepted the Offer: Don Fernand de Cardonne said, He had rather Converse with me than Play: so the three others began, and I for some time gave myself over to the looking on them, with great Pleasure, for their Way is quite different from ours;

ours: They never utter a word; I do not fay, to complain, (for this would be unworthy the Spanifh Gravity) but to demand a gano, or to cut higher, or to fhew that one may take fome other Advantage: In a word, they feem to be Statues, or Pieces of German Clockwork, never appearing tranfported with either good or bad Luck. Among other Difcourfe which I had with D. Fred. de Cardonne, he told me, There were two obfervable things in Catalonia, one of which is a Mountain of Salt, partly white as Snow, and the other part clearer and more tranfparent than Chryftal: that there is Blue, Green, Violet, Orange, and a thoufand different Colours, which yet lofes its tincture when wetted; it continually forms itfelf, and grows there: and though commonly the places where Salt is to be found, are fo barren, that you fee not fo much as an Herb, yet there are here Pine-Trees of great height, and
excel-

excellent Vineyards: When the Sun darts its Rays on this Mountain, it looks as if it wholly confifted of the moft precious Stones in the World: but the beft of it is, that it yields a good Revenue.

The other Particular he mentioned to me, was of a Fountain, whofe Water is very good, and of the fame Coulour as Claret: 'I have never heard any thing of this,' faid I to him, 'but one of my Relations, who has been in Catalonia, has affured me there is a Fountain near Balut, whofe Water is as others are for Colour, and yet whatever you put therein, appears like Gold.' 'I have feen it, Madam,' continued Don Frederic; 'and I remember a Man that was very covetous, and more foolifh, went thither every Day to put therein his Silver, hoping in time 'twould be chang'd into Gold; but he was fo far from enriching himfelf that he was ruin'd; for fome Peafants, more fubtle and crafty

crafty than he, having perceived what he did, ſtood watching a little lower, and the Stream of the Water would now and then bring ſome Pieces to them. If you return into France by Catalonia,' added he, 'you will ſee this Fountain,' 'It is not that which can draw me thither,' reply'd I, 'but the deſire of paſſing by Montferat, wou'd make me undertake a longer Journey.' 'It is ſituated,' ſaid he, 'near Barcelona, and is a place of great Devotion: It ſeems as if the Rock were ſawed through the middle; the Church ſtands high, is ſmall and obſcure. By the help of the Fourſcore and Ten Lamps of Silver, you perceive the Image of the Virgin, which looks very duskiſh, and is held for miraculous. The Altar coſt Philip the Second thirty thouſand Crowns; and here is every Day ſeen Pilgrims from all Parts of the World; this Holy Place abounds with Hermitages, inhabited by Perſons of great Devotion: Theſe

These are commonly Men of good Birth, who have not left the World till they have well tryed it, and who appear much taken with the Sweets of their Retirements, though the Place be difmal; and 'twould been impoffible to have had accefs to it, had not a Paffage been cut through the Rocks. Yet you find here feveral agreeable Objects, a curious Profpect, various Springs, Gardens well dreft by thefe Religiofes own hands, and every where a certain Air of Solitude and Devotion, which mightily affects thofe who come there. We have another famous place of Devotion,' added he, ' and that is Nueftra Senora del Pilar: it is at Saragoffa, in a Chappel on a Pillar of Marble, where our Lady holds the Babe Jefus in her Arms. It is pretended, that the Virgin appeared on this fame Pillar to St. James; and the Image is here worfhipt with great Reverence. It cannot be well obferv'd, becaufe it ftands fo high, and in a

very

very dark place; fo that without the Flambeaux it could not be feen at all. Here are always Fifty Lamps burning; Gold and precious Stones fhine here on all fides; and the Pilgrims come here in great Sholes. But yet,' fays he, 'I may truly fay, in favour of Saragoffa that 'tis one of the fineft Towns you fhall fee; it is fituated along the Ebre, in a vaft Field, is adorn'd with great Buildings, rich Churches, a ftately Bridge, fine open Places, and the moft charming Women in the World, who love French, and will omit nothing to oblige you to fpeak well of 'em, if you pafs by there.' I told him, I had already heard feveral things fpoken of them to their commendation: 'But,' continu'd I, 'this Country is very Barren, and the Souldiers can hardly fubfift in it.' 'In effect,' replied he, 'whether the Air be bad, or that they want Neceffaries, the Flemmings and Germans cannot live there; and if they do not die ' there,

there, 'tis becaufe they run away. The Spaniards and Neopolitans are more prone than they to defert; thefe laft pafs through France, to return into their Country; the others Coaft the Pyrenees along Languedoc, and enter Caftille by Navarre, or Bifcaye. This is a Courfe which the old Souldiers fail not to fteer; for the new-rais'd ones, they perifh in Catalonia, being not accuftomed thereto; and 'tis certain there's no place where War is more troublefome to the King of Spain: He maintains his Forces here with great Charge, and the Advantage which the Enemy gains of him is not fmall; and I very well know they are more fenfible at Madrid for the fmalleft Lofs in Catalonia, than they would be for the greateft in Flanders, or Milan, or elfe-where. But at prefent,' continues he, 'we are going to be more at our Eafe than we have been, being expected at Court, that the Peace will be lafting, becaufe they

they talk much of a Marriage which will make a new Alliance; and the Marquefs de Los Balbares, Plenipotentiary at Nimiguen, has receiv'd Orders to pafs fpeedily to France, to demand of that King, Mademoifelle d' Orleans; therefore it is not doubted but the Marriage will be concluded: But it is thought very ftrange, Don John of Auftria fhould confent to this Marriage.'
'You will do me a fingular Pleafure,' faid I, interrupting him, 'if you would inform me of fome Particularities touching this Prince: It is natural for to have a Curiofity in relation to Perfons of this Character; and when a body comes into a Court where one was never before, that I may not appear a Novice, I fhould have fome previous Notices.' He anfwered me, It would be a great fatisfaction to him, if he could relate any thing might pleafe me; and he began thus:

'You will not, perhaps, Madam, think it amifs, that I begin at the Original

iginal of Things, and tell you, That this Prince was Son of one of the fineſt Women in Spain, named Maria Calderona; ſhe was a Player, and the Duke de Medina de las Torres became deſperately in love with her: This Cavalier had ſo many Advantages above others, that Calderonna lov'd him no leſs than ſhe was beloved by him. In the Heat of this Intrigue, Philip the Fourth ſaw her, and preferr'd her to one of the Queen's Maids of Honour, and who was ſo griev'd at this Change of the King, whom ſhe really loved, and had a Son by, that ſhe retired from the World, and betook herſelf to Las del Calſas Reales, where ſhe put on the Religio's Habit. As for Calderonne, her inclination lying wholly towards the Duke de Medina, ſhe would not hearken to the King, without the Duke would thereto conſent: She ſpake to him of it, and offered to withdraw ſecretly where he would; but the Duke fearing to incur the

the King's Difpleafure, anfwer'd her, He was refolv'd to yield up to His Majefty a Treafure which he was not in a Capacity to contend for. She made him a thoufand Reproaches for this; fhe call'd him Traytor to his Love, ingrateful towards his Miftrefs: And moreover, told him, That though he was fo Happy as that he could difpofe of his Heart as he pleafed, yet fhe could not do the fame; and therefore he muft continue to vifit her, or prepare to fee her die with Defpair. The Duke affected with fo great a Paffion, promifed to feign a Journey to Andaloufia, and to remain with her hid in a Clofet: he effectually parted from the Court, and afterwards fhut himfelf up (as it was agreed) whatever Rifque he ran by fo imprudent Conduct. The King, in the mean time, was very Amorous, and remain'd very well fatisfi'd: She had, during this, Don John d'Auftria, and the Refemblance he had with the

Duke

Duke de Medina de Las Torres, had made it be thought that he was his Son; but tho' the King had other Children, and particularly the Bishop of Malaga, good Fortune decided in his Favour, and he has been only acknowledg'd.

'Don John's Friends say, That 'twas by reason of the Exchange which had been made of the Son of Calderonna, for the Son of Queen Elizabeth; and here's how they set forth this Change, which is a Story made on purpose to impose on the World, and which I believe has no ground of Truth: They pretend, the King being desperately in love with this Player, she became big with Child at the same time as the Queen; and seeing the King's Passion was so greatly towards her, that she might expect any thing, she so ordered it, that she made him promise her, That if the Queen had a Son, and she likewise, he should put hers in his place: " What will you lose by this,

this, Sir?" said she, "Will it not be your Son that will still Reign, only with this difference, that loving me, as you say you do, you will love him likewise the better." She had Wit, and the King could deny her nothing; he consented, and in effect the Business was manag'd with that Address, that the Queen being brought to Bed of a Son, and Calderonna of another, the Exchange was made. He that should have Reign'd, and who bore the Name of Baltazar, died at the Age of fourteen Years: The King was told, 'twas with over-heating himself at Tennis; but the truth is, this Prince was suffered to keep bad Company, which procured for him his Misfortunes; it is said likewise, That Don Pedro d'Arragon, his Governour, and Chief Gentleman of his Chamber, more contributed to this than any other, suffering him to bring into his Apartment a Woman he lov'd; after this he was taken with a violent Fever,

Fever, and conceal'd the Occafion: The Phificians who were ignorant of it, thought to eafe him by frequent Bleedings, which put an end to what ftrength he had; and by this means they ended his Life. The King knowing, but too late, what had hapn'd, banifht Don Pedro for not hindring this Excefs, or for not having timely difcover'd it.

'In the mean time Don John of Auftria, who was brought up as the Natural Son, chang'd not his Condition, though this ought to have been, had he been indeed the lawful Son; yet notwithftanding this, his Creatures affirm, He fo exactly refembles Q. Elizabeth, that fhe needs no other Picture of her Likenefs. And this Opinion fails not of gaining Belief with the People, who run violently after Novelties, and who fo Paffionately loved this great Queen, that they bewail her ftill as if fhe was but now deceas'd. It is true, that if Don John
of

of Auſtria would make his Advantage of the favourable Diſpoſitions of the People, he has met with ſeveral Opportunities of extending his Fortune very far; but his only Aim is to ſerve the King, and to keep his Subjects in thoſe Sentiments of Fidelity they ought to have for him.

'To return to Calderonna: The King ſurprized one day the Duke de Medina with her, and in the exceſs of his Rage, he ran to him with his Poynard in his Hand; he was about to kill him, when this Woman placed herſelf between, telling him, He might ſtrike her if he would. Having the moſt extream Paſſion for her, he could not but Pardon him, contenting himſelf only with baniſhing him: But underſtanding ſhe continu'd to love him, and write to him, he ſtudied only how to get a new Paſſion; when he had one ſtrong enough not to apprehend the Charms of Calderonna, he ſent word to her to retire into a Mon-

Monaſtery, as is cuſtomary when the King forſakes his Miſtreſs. She put it not off, writing a Letter to the Duke, to bid him Adieu: And ſhe receiv'd the Veil of a Religio from the Hand of the Apoſtolick Nuncio, who became ſince Innocent X. It is very likely the King believ'd Don John was his real Son, ſeeing he loved him ſo dearly: One thing will appear to you very ſingular, which is, that a King of Spain having Natural Sons owned by him, they never enter Madrid during his Life: So Don John was brought up at Ocanna, which is ſome Leagues diſtant from it. The King, his Father, came oft thither, and he made him come even to the Gates of the Town, where he went to meet him. This Cuſtom comes from that the Grandees of Spain diſpute the Rank which theſe Princes would hold. Don John, before he went into Catalonia, remain'd commonly at Buen Retiro, which is a Royal Seat, at one

of

of the fartheſt parts of Madrid, a little without the Gate: And he ſhew'd himſelf ſo little, that he was never ſeen at any Publick Feaſt during the Life of the late King: but ſince, Times have chang'd, and his Fortunes ſtand on a different bottom.

'Whilſt the Queen, Maria Ann of Auſtria, Siſter to the Emperour, and the King's Mother, Govern'd Spain; and her Son was not yet of Age to hold the Reigns of the State. She would have always Don John keep from the Court; and moreover, found herſelf ſo capable of Governing, that ſhe had a mind to eaſe her Son for a long time of the Burden of Ruling. She was not troubled to ſee him ignorant of whatever might give a deſire of Reigning: but though ſhe brought the greateſt Pre-cautions, to hinder him from feeling he was under too ſtrict a Tutelage, and ſuffered no Perſons to come near him, but thoſe ſhe was well aſſured of; yet this hindred not

not but some of the King's Faithful Servants hazarded themselves, by giving him to understand what he might do for his Liberty. He follow'd the Advice was given him; and in fine, having taken Measures accordingly, he stole away one Night, and went to Buen Retiro. He as soon sent from thence an Order to the Queen his Mother, not to stir out of the Palace.

'Don John is of a middle Stature, well-shaped, Black and lively Eyes, and a most Manly Countenance. He is Polite, Generous, and very Brave. He is ignorant of nothing befitting his Birth, being well-verst in all Arts and Sciences. He writes and speaks very well Five Languages, and understands yet more. He has for a long time studied Judicial Astrology. There is no Instrument which he cannot make, and use with the best Masters. He works on all kinds of Mechanicks, makes Arms, and paints finely. He took a great Pleasure in the Mathematicks;

maticks; but being charg'd with the Government of the State, he has been oblig'd to lay afide all other Employments.

'He came to Buen-Retiro in the beginning of the Year 1677, and as foon as he was there, he fent the Queen-Mother to Toledo, becaufe fhe had declared againft him, and hindred his return to the King. Don John had an extream Joy in receiving from the King's own Hand an Order to take Care of Every thing, and to manage the Affairs of the Kingdom: And 'twas not without occafion he difcharged himfelf on him, feeing he then was ignorant of the Art of Reigning. It was alledg'd for a Reafon of his flow Education, That the King his Father was dying when he gave him Life: That when he came into the World, they were fain to put him in a Box of Cotten, being fo tender and fmall, that he could not be fwadled: That he was brought up in the Arms,
and

and on the Knees of the Ladies of the Palace, till he was Ten Years old, without putting his Foot once all this while on the Ground to walk: That in the Sequel the Queen his Mother, who was engaged by all the Ties of Natural Duty to preserve this only Heir of the Spanish Branch, fearing to lose him, dared not let him study, left by too great an Application he should lose his Health, which in truth was very unsound: And 'twas observ'd, that the great Number of Women, with whom the King always was, and who too sharply reprehended him for his Faults which he committed, had inspired him with such a great Aversion to them, that as soon as ever he had notice a Lady staid for him in any place he was to pass, he stole another way, or kept himself shut up all day in his Chamber. The Marchioness de Luz Veles, who was his Governess, told me, she waited for an Opportunity full six months to speak with

with him, and when Chance had brought them unavoidably to him, he took their Requeſts from their Hands, but turn'd his Head another way, for fear he ſhould ſee them. His Health is ſince ſo increaſed, that his Marriage with the Arch-Dutcheſs, the Emperor's Daughter, having been broke off by Don John, by reaſon 'twas the Queen-Mothers Project, he has deſired to marry Mademoiſelle d' Orleans. The Circumſtances of the Peace which are lately concluded at Nimiguen, made him caſt his Eyes towards this Princeſs, with whoſe excellent Qualities, Madam, you are better acquainted than I.

'It is hard to believe, that having Diſpoſitions ſo far from Gallantry, he ſhould become ſo ſuddenly and vehemently in love with the Queen, as he became on the only Rehearſal of her good Qualities, and at the ſight of her Picture in Minature, which was ſhew'd him. He never lets it go out of his Hand;

Hand; he always holds it to his Heart; He Dialogues with it so prettily, as astonishes all the Courtiers; for he speaks a Language he never spoke: His Passion for the Princess furnishes him with a thousand Thoughts, which he dares not entrust any body with. He thinks no body makes haste enough; and therefore sends fresh Curriers every day to carry his Billets doux, and bring back News of her.

'When you come to Madrid,' added he, 'you will hear, Madam, several Particulars which have without doubt hapned since I was there, and which will perhaps more satisfie your Curiosity than what I have related to you.' 'I am very much oblig'd to you,' answer'd I, 'for your Civilities; but do me the Favour to oblige me farther, in giving me the true Character of the Spaniards: You know them, and I am perswaded nothing has escap'd your Enquiries; You speaking to me without Passion and Interest, I may
reckon

reckon my felf fure of what you tell me.' 'Why believe you, Madam,' replied he fmiling, 'that I fhall fpeak to you more fincerely than another? There are Reafons which may render me fufpected: They are my Mafters; I muft manage them; And if I be not Politick enough to do it, the Vexation of being conftrained to obey them, would tempt me to entertain Notions in their Refpect contrary to Truth.' 'However it be,' faid I, interrupting him, 'pray tell me what you know of them.'

'The Spaniards,' faid he, 'have always paft for Fierce and Glorious: This Glory is mixt with Gravity; and they carry it fo far, that one may call it an extravagant Pride: They are Brave, without being Rafh; yet they are accufed for not being daring enough. They are Cholerick, Revengeful, without fhewing any Tranfport, Liberal without Oftentation, fober in their diet, very Prefumptuous in Profperity, too
Ram-

Rampant in Adverfity: They Idolize Women; they are fo prepoffeft in their Favour, that they fhew no Difcretion in the Choice of their Wives: They are Patient to Excefs, Obftinate, Idle, Singular, Philofophifers: And as to the reft, Men of Honour, keeping their Words, tho it coft 'em their Lives. They have a great deal of Wit and Vivacity, eafily comprehend, explain themfelves in the fame manner, and in few Words; They are Prudent, Jealous without meafure, Difinterefted, bad Oeconomifts, Clofe, Superftitious, great Catholicks, at leaft in appearance: They are good Poets, and write Verfes with great Facility. They would be capable of Nobler Sciences, would they vouchfafe to apply themfelves thereto.

'They have a Greatnefs of Soul, Elevated Wit, Conftancy, a Natural Serioufnefs, and a Refpect for Ladies, as is not feen elfewhere: They have a Set-Behaviour, full of Affectation, intoxicated

toxicated with their own Merit, hardly ever in this Particular doing Right to that of others. Their Bravery confifts in ftanding Valiantly on the Defenfive Part, without giving Ground, and without dreading Danger; but they love not to feek it, which proceeds from their great Judgment: They difcern Danger, and avoid it. Their greateft Defect, in my Opinion, is the Paffion of Revenge, and the Means they ufe for this: Their Maxims hereupon are abfolutely oppofite to Chriftianity and Honour: When they have receiv'd an Affront, they make him be Affaffinated who has offered it. They are not contented with this; for they caufe them to be Affaffinated likewife whom they have offended, in the Apprehenfion of being prevented, knowing well, that if they do not kill, they fhall be kill'd themfelves. They pretend to juftifie themfelves herein, when they fay, That their Enemy having took the firft Advantage,

tage, they ought to secure themselves of the second: That should they fail herein, they would wrong their Reputation: That you must not fight with a Man that has insulted over you, but put your self in a Condition to punish him, without running half the Danger. It is true, that Impunity authorises this Conduct; for the Priviledge of Churches and Convents in Spain, is to give an assured Retreat to Criminals; And as near as they can, they commit these Villanies hard by a Sanctuary, to have the less way to an Altar; Which you see oft embraced by a Villain, with his Poynard reeking in his Hand, and be-smeared with the Blood of the Murther which he has committed.

'As to their Persons, they are very lean, little, fine shape, comely Head, good Faces, fine Eyes, well-set Teeth, yellow and duskish Complexion; they will have one walk slowly, commend big Legs, and a little Foot, Shooes without Heels, parting the Hair on both

both fides, being ftrait cut, and kept behind their Ears with a great Two-handed Hat, an Habit always Black, inftead of a Shirt, Taffity Sleeves, or black Tabby, a Sword of a ftrange length, with a black Freize Cloak over all this, very ftrait Breeches, hanging Sleeves, and a Poynard. All this muft fo dif-figure a Man, let him be otherwife never fo well-fhaped, that they feem to affect a Garb the moft difagreeable; And ones Eyes cannot with any Complacency accuftom themfelves to this fight.'

Don Frederick would have continued on his Difcourfe, and I had fo much pleafure in hearing him, that I would not have interrupted him; but he broke off himfelf, having obferv'd that the Play was at an end, and confidering, that we were to fet out early next Morning, he thought I might be defirous of retiring; he therefore with the other Gentlemen, bad me good Night. I rofe in effect very foon next

next Morning, becaufe 'twas a great Journey to Birbiefca, where we intended to lie. We follow'd the River to avoid the Mountains, and paſt at Oron, a great River, which falls into the Ebre. We a while after entred into fo ftrait a Way, that our Litters could fcaace pafs: We afcended along a very ftrait Coaft to Pancorvo, whofe Caftle I faw ftanding on a rais'd Ground, not far diftant: We traverft a great Plain; and this was a Novelty to us, to fee an even Country: This here is furrounded with feveral Mountains, which feem linkt together as a Chain, and efpecially thofe of Occa: We muft again pafs over a little River, before we can come to Birbiefca: This is only a Borough, which has nothing remarkable but its Colledge, and fome few pleafant Gardens along the Water. But I may fay, we came thither in worfe Weather than any we had yet: I was fo tired, that as foon as I arriv'd I went to Bed: fo that I faw saw not Don Fernand de Toledo, and the other Gentlemen, till the next Day, at Caſtel de Peones. But I ſhould tell you how one is ſerv'd in theſe Inns, they being all alike: When you come into one of them, wearied and tired, roaſted by the heat of the Sun, or frozen by the Snows (for there is ſeldom any Temperament between theſe Two Extreams), you ſee neither Pot on the Fire, nor Plates waſh'd: You enter into the Stable, and from thence to your Chamber; this Stable is ordinarily full of Mules and Muletteers, who make uſe of their Mules Saddles for Pillows in the night, and in the day-time they ſerve 'em for Tables: They eat very friendly with their Mules, and are very good Company together.

The Stair-Caſe by which you go up is very ſtrait, and does rather reſemble a ſorry Ladder: La Sennoro de la Caſa receives you with her Gown tuckt up, and her dangling Sleeves; ſhe takes time

time to put on her Sunday-Cloathes, whilſt you get out of your Litter: and ſhe never omits this; for they are all very Poor and Vain Glorious. You are ſhewed a Chamber, whoſe Walls are white enough, hung with a thouſand little ſcurvy Pictures of Saints; the Beds are without Curtains, the Covertures of Cotton, the Sheets as large as Napkins, and the Napkins like Pocket-handkerchiefs; and you muſt be in ſome conſiderable Town to find four or five of them; for in other places there are none, no more than there are Forks: They have only a Cup in the Houſe; and if the Mule-Drivers get firſt hold of it, which commonly happens, if they pleaſe, (for they are ſerv'd with more Reſpect than thoſe whom they bring) you muſt ſtay patiently till they have done with it, or drink out of an Earthen Pitcher. It is impoſſible to warm one at the Kitchin-fire, without being choaked, for they have no Chimneys;
and

and 'tis the fame in all the Houfes on the Road; there is an Hole made in the top of the Ceiling, and the Smoak goes out thence; the Fire is in the midft of the Kitchin: They put what you would have roafted on Tiles, and when 'tis well gril'd on one fide, they turn the other: when 'tis grofs Meat, they faften it to a String, and fo let it hang on the Fire, and turn it with their Hands; fo that the Smoak makes it fo black, that it would turn ones Stomach to look on it.

I think there cannot be a better Reprefentation of Hell than thefe fort of Kitchins, and the Perfons in them; for not to fpeak of this horrible Smoak, which blinds and choaks one, they are a Dozen of Men, and as many Women, blacker than Devils, nafty and ftinking like Swine, and clad like Beggars. There are always fome of 'em impudently grating on a forry Guitar, and finging like a Cat a roafting. The Women have all of 'em
their

their Hair about their Ears, and you would take 'em for Bedlamites; they have Glafs Necklaces, which hang twifted about their Necks like Ropes of Onions, but however ferve to cover the Naftinefs of their Skin. They are as great Thieves as any are in Jayls, and they are urgent to ferve you only to have an opportunity to fteal fomething of you, though it be but a Pin.

Before all things, the Miftrefs of the Houfe brings you her little Children, who are bareheaded in the midft of Winter, though but of a Day old: fhe makes 'em touch your Cloaths, fhe rubs their Eyes with them, their Cheeks, Throat, and Hands. This feems as if one was become a Relick, and could heal all Difeafes. Thefe Ceremonies over, you are askt, If you will eat any thing; and though at Mid-night, you muft fend to the Butchery, the Market, the Tavern, the Bakers; in fine, to all parts of the Town,

Town, to gather wherewith to make a forry Meal. For though the Mutton here be very tender, their way of frying it with Oyl, is not to every Bodies Relifh. Here are great ftore of Partridges, and thofe very large; they are not very fat, but dry; and to make 'em drier, they roaft 'em to a Coal. The Pidgeons here are excellent; and in feveral places here is good Fifh, efpecially Beffugoffes, which have the tafte of a Trout, and of which they make Pafties, which would be good, were they not ftuff'd with Garlick, Saffron, and Pepper. Their Bread is white enough, and fweet, that one would think it made up with Sugar; but it is ill wrought, and fo little baked, that it is as heavy as Lead in the Stomach: it has the fhape of a flat Cake, and is not much thicker than one's finger. The Wine is good, and Fruits in their feafon, efpecially Grapes, which are very large, and of delicate tafte. You may reckon yourfelf certain

tain of a good Defart. You have Sallads here of fuch good Lettice as the World cannot afford better.

Do not think (Dear Coufin) 'tis fufficient to fay, Go fetch fuch things, to have them; for not very feldom you can meet with nothing: But fuppofing you find what you would have, you muft give out your Money beforehand: fo that your Meat is paid for before you have begun to eat it; for the Mafter of the Inn is only allowed to Lodge you: they alledge for a Reafon, That it is not juft one only Perfon fhould go away with all the Profit from Travellers, it being better the Money fhould be difperfed.

You enter not any Inn to Dine, but carry your Provifion with you, and ftop at the Bank of fome River, where the Mule-Drivers bate their Mules; and this is with Oats or Barley, with chopt Straw, which they carry with them in great Sacks; for as to Hay they give 'em none. It is not allow'd

a

a Woman to tarry above two Days in an Inn on the Road, unlefs fhe can offer good Reafons. And here's enough in relation to Inns, and the Manner of your Treatment therein.

After Supper thefe Gentlemen play'd at Ombre, and I not being ftrong enough to play againft them, I went fhares with Don Frederic de Cardonne; and Don Fernand drew near the Fire-fide to me; he told me, He could have wifht my time would permit me to pafs by Vailladolid; that it is the moft pleafant Town of Old Caftille, it having been for a great while the Manfion of the Kings of Spain; and that they have a Palace there fit for them. That as to him, he had Relations there would be infinitely pleafed to Entertain me; and would fhew me the Dominicans Church, which the Dukes of Lerma have founded; that it was very Stately, and the Portal of fingular Beauty, by means of the Figures and Emboffed Work, which enrich it:
That

That in the Colledge of the same Convent the French see there with great satisfaction, all the Walls full of Flower de Luces; it being said, a Bishop who depended on the King of France, had been at the Charge of Painting them. He added, They would have carried me to the Religioses of St. Claire, to shew me in the Choir of their Church, the Tomb of a Castillan Knight, whence 'tis said, issues out Accents and Groans every time any of his Family are near their Deaths. I smiled at this, as being doubtful of the Truth of such kind of Relations: 'You give not Credit to what I say,' continued he, 'neither would I engage for the Truth of it, though all the Country thereabouts are so fully perswaded of it, that you would be suspected for an Heretick should you question it. But it is certain there is a Bell in Arragon, in a small Town call'd Villilla, on the Ebre, which is about fifty Foot compass, and it happens

pens fometimes to found of itfelf, it being not perceiveable to be agitated by any Winds or Earthquakes: In a word, by no vifible thing. It firft Tolls, and afterwards, by intervals, Rings out, as well in the Day as the Night: When it is heard, it is not doubted but it denounces fome fad Accident; which is what happened in 1601, on Thursday the 13th of June, till Saturday the 15th of the fame Month; it ceafed then to Ring, but it began again on Corpus Chrifti, when they were on the point of making the Proceffion. It was heard likewife when Alphonfus the Fifth, K. of Arragon, went into Italy to take Poffeffion of the Kingdom of Naples. It was heard at the Death of Charles the Fifth. It denoted the Departure of Don Sebaftion, King of Portugal, for Africk. The Extremity of King Philip the Second: and the Deceafe of his laft Wife Q. Ann.' 'You would have me to believe you, Don Fernand,' faid I;

I; 'Perhaps I shall seem too obstinate in standing out all this while, but you will agree these are Matters one may lawfully doubt of.' 'Nay, Madam,' replied he, with a pleasant Air, 'I tell you nothing but what I can have a thousand Witnesses to justifie; but perhaps you will sooner believe Don Esteve de Carvajal in a thing as extraordinary in his Country.' He at the same time call'd to him, demanding of him, 'Whether 'twere not true, that there is in the Convent of Cordoüa a Clock which fails not to Ring every time a Religious is to die; so that the time is known to a Day?' Don Esteve confirm'd what Don Fernand said: and though I remain'd not absolutely convinc'd, yet I made a shew as if I was.

'You pass so quickly through Old Castille,' continued Don Fernand, 'that you will not have time to see what's most remarkable: The Picture of the Blessed Virgin is talkt of far and near,

near, which was found miraculously ſtampt on a Rock; it belongs to the Religio's Auguſtines d' Avila, and several Perſons go there out of Devotion; but one has no leſs Curioſity to ſee certain Mines of Salt, which are near there, in a village call'd Mengraville; you deſcend above two hundred Steps under Ground, and then enter into a vaſt Cavern form'd by Nature, whoſe Top, or Roof, is upheld by one only Pillar of Chryſtalin Salt, of aſtoniſhing Largeneſs and Colour. Near this place, in the Town of Soria, you ſee a great Bridge without a River, and a great River without a Bridge, the River being forc'd out of its place by an Earthquake.

'But if you go as far as Medina del Campo,' added he, 'I am ſure the Inhabitants will give you a welcome Entrance, only becauſe you are of the French Nation, whom they much affect, to diſtinguiſh themſelves hereby from the Sentiments of the other Caſtil-

Medina del Campo

ment, which was found miraculously Cramp'd on a Rock; it belongs to the Religious Augustines d'Arles, and several Fathers go there out of Devotion; but one has no less Curiosity to see certain Mines of Salt, which are near Goula, in a village call'd Marganville; you descend above two hundred Steps under Ground, and then enter into a vast Cavern form'd by Nature, whose Roof, as 'twere, is upheld by one only Pillar of Chrystaline Salt of astonishing Largeness and Lustre. Near this place, in the Tower of Scatta, you see a great Bridge without a River, and a great River without a Bridge, the River being forc'd out of its place by an Earthquake.

But if you go as far as Medina del Campo," added he, "I am sure the Inhabitants will give you a welcome Entrance, only because you are of the French Nation, whom they much affect, to distinguish themselves hereby from the Sentiments of the other Castil-

Castillians: Their Town is so priviledg'd that the K. of Spain has not the Power to create any Officers, nor the Pope to confer Benefices: this Right belongs to the Townsmen, and they often fall together by the Ears, in the chusing of their Magistrates and Ecclesiasticks.

'One of the Rarities of this Country is the Aquaduct of Segovia, which is five Leagues in length; it has above two hundred Arches of extraordinary heighth, tho' in several places there are two standing on one another; and 'tis all built on Free Stone, there having been no Mortar, or any Cement to joyn them: This is lookt on as one of the Romans Works, or at least as worthy to be so. The River which is at the end of the Town surrounds the Castle, and serves it for a Ditch; it is built on a Rock. Among several things remarkable, you see the Effigies of the Kings of Spain, who have Reign'd for several Years: And there is is no Town but Segovia and Seville where Money is Coyned, and the Pieces of Eight which are made at the former Places are held to be the beſt; and this is by means of the River which turns certain Mills that ſtamp the Money. Here are likewiſe moſt curious Walks along a Meadow planted with Elm Trees, whoſe Leaves are ſo thick and large, that the greateſt Heats of the Sun cannot pierce them.' 'I want not Curioſity,' ſaid I to him, 'for all things which deſerve it; but I at preſent want Time to ſee them: However, I ſhould be very glad to arrive timely at Burgos, to view the Town.' 'Which is to ſay, Madam,' replied Don Fernand, 'we muſt loſe your Company, and let you retire.'

He gave notice thereof to the other Gentlemen, who gave over their Play, and we thus ſeparated.

I roſe this Morning before Day; and I end this Letter at Burgos, where I now

now arrived: Thus, Dear Coufin, I fhall fend you nothing of this Day, but fhall take the firft occafion to acquaint you with what befals me.

Yours.

From Burgos,
 Feb. 27, 1673.

Letter IV

WE could sensibly perceive in arriving at Burgos, that this Town is colder than any of those we past; and 'tis likewise said, you have none of those excessive Heats which are intollerable in other Parts of Spain: The Town stands where you descend the Mountain, and reaches to the Plain as far as the River, which washes the foot of the Wall: the Streets are very strait and even: the Castle is not great, but very strong, and is seen on the top of the Mountain: A little lower is the Triumphant Arch of Fernando Gonsales, which the Curious do much admire. This Town was the first that was conquer'd from the Mores; and the Kings of Spain have long resided here; 'tis the Capital

tal of Old Caſtille; it holds the firſt Rank in the two States of the two Caſtilles, although Toledo diſputes it with her: You ſee her fine Buildings; and Velaſco's Palace is very ſtately. Here are in all the broad Streets and ſpacious Places, Fountains, with Statues, ſome of which are good Pieces; but the fineſt ſight is the Cathedral, which is ſo large, that Maſs is ſaid in five ſeveral places of it, without any diſturbance to each other: the Architecture is ſo exquiſitely wrought, that it may paſs among the Gothick Buildings for a Maſter-Piece of Art: and this is ſo much the more remarkable, in that they build very ſorrily in Spain; in ſome places this is through Poverty, and in others want of Stone and Lime: I am told that even at Madrid you ſee Houſes of Earth, and the fineſt are made with Brick, cemented with the ſame, for want of Lime. To paſs from the Town to the Suburbs of Bega, you
go

go over three Stone Bridges: the Gate which anfwers that of Santa Maria, ftands high, with the Image of the Virgin upon it: this Suburb contains the greateft part of the Convents and Hofpitals; there is a great one founded by Philip the Second, to receive the Pilgrims which go to St. James, and which entertains them for a Day. The Abbey of Mille Flores, whofe Building is very ftately, is not far diftant. You fee here in this Suburb feveral Gardens which are watered with Fountains and pleafant Springs; the River ferves for a Channel: And you find in a great Park inclofed with Walls, pleafant Walks at all times of the Year.

I would have feen the Crucifix in the Auguftines Convent; it is placed in a Chappel of the Cloyfter, large and dark enough, fo that you could hardly difcern it, were it not for the Lamps, which are continually burning, they'r above an hundred; fome are of Gold, and

and others of Silver, of so extraordinary a size, that they cover all the Vault of this Chappel: there are sixty Silver candlesticks of a length exceeding the tallest Man, and so heavy that two Men cannot lift 'em: they stand on the ground on both sides of the Altar; those which are upon it are of Massy Gold: You see between 'em two Crosses of the same, set out with Precious Stones, and Crowns hanging over the Altar, adorn'd with Pearls and Diamonds of great Lustre: The Chappel is hung with Tapistry, wrought with Gold; it is so laden with rich Gifts, that there's hardly room to put 'em in; so that part of 'em are kept in the Treasury.

The Holy Crucifix stands on the Altar, near the natural bigness, it is covered with three Curtains one on another, all embroidered with Pearls and Diamonds: When they open them, which is not done without great Ceremony, and for Persons of Quality,

Quality, feveral Bells are rung, every one falls on his Knees: and it muft be granted, that this place and fight ftrikes one with an Awful Regard: The Crucifix is of Carv'd Work, and cannot be better made; its Carnation is very natural; it is covered from the Breafts to the Feet with a fine Linnen, in feveral Foulds or Pleats, which makes it look like a loofe Jerkin, which in my Opinion, is not over-agreeable.

It is commonly held, that Nicodemus made it; but thofe who are for making every thing Miraculous, will have it brought down from Heaven, they know not how nor when. I was told, certain Monks of this Town had once ftole it, and convey'd it away; but it took a convenient time to give 'em the flip, and was found the next Morning in the Chappel in its ufual place: Thefe honeft People being enraged, that it fhould ferve 'em fuch a Trick, muftered up their Forces, and

and violently laid Hands on't the second time, but to as little purpose; for 'twould by no means stay with 'em: However, it works Miracles, and is one of the chief Objects of Devotion in Spain: The Religious tell you, it sweats every Friday.

I was going into my Inn, when we saw the Sieur de Cardonne's Valet de Chambre, running as fast as he could after us; he was booted, and three Friers scowring after him: I was over-rash in my Judgment; for I could not but think he had stole something in this rich Chappel, and was taken in the Fact; but his Master, who was with me, having demanded of him, What put him on such full speed? He answer'd, He went into the Chappel of the Holy Crucifix with his Spurs on, and the Fryers had kept him in custody, to get Money of him, but that he was gotten out of their Clutches, but they were now upon the Hunt for him. They make it a
Forfeit,

Forfeit, as well as others, for a Man to go with Spurs into thefe Holy Places.

The Town is not very great; it is adorned with a fpacious Place; here are high Pillars which bear up very fine Lodgings. The Bull-Feafts are kept here; for the People are much delighted with this fort of Divertifement. There is alfo a very well-built Bridge, long and large: the River which paffes under it, bathes a Meadow, on the Bank of which you fee Allies of Trees, which form a moft delicious Walk. Trade was heretofore confiderable, but it is of late much diminifht. The beft Caftillan is here fpoken; and the Men are naturally Souldiers, fo that when the King has need of them, he finds here great Numbers, and better Men than elfewhere.

After Supper our Company fet to Play, as heretofore: Don Sancho Sanniento was for yielding his place to any one, pretending 'twas his Right
to

to Entertain me this Evening. I knew he had lately return'd from Sicily; I askt him, Whether he had been one of thofe who had help'd to Chaftize thofe Rebellious People? 'Alas, Madam,' faid he, 'the Marquefs de Las Navas was fufficient to punifh them beyond what their Crime deferv'd: I was at Naples, in the defign to pafs into Flanders, where I have Relations of the fame Name. The Marquefs de Los Veles, Vice-Roy of Naples, engaged me to leave my firft Project, and embark myfelf with the Marquefs de Las Navas, whom the King fent into Sicily: We fet Sail in two Veffels of Majorca, and arrived at Meffina the fixth of January. Having fent no notice of his coming, and no body expecting it, he was not receiv'd with the Honours paid commonly to the Vice-Roys: But in truth, his Intentions were fo cruel againft thefe poor People, that his Entrance fhould have been made in Tears.

'Scarcely

'Scarcely was he arriv'd, but he clapt up the two Sheriffs in Prifon, named Vicenzo Zuffo, and Don Diego: He put Spaniards in their Places; he rigoroufly abolifht the Colledge of Knights of the Star; and began to execute the Orders which Gonzaga had long receiv'd, and which he had eluded through Favour or Weaknefs. He immediately publifht an Order, by which the King chang'd all the Form of Government of Meffina, depriv'd the Town of its Revenues, forbad its bearing for the future the Glorious Title of Exemplary, diffolved the Senate, and put into the place of fix Sheriffs, fix Officers, two of which fhould be Spaniards; that these Officers fhould not for the future appear in Publick with their Formalities; that they fhould no more be preceded by Drums and Trumpets, ride no more together in a Coach with four Horfes, as they were wont; that they fhould fit henceforward on a plain Bench;

Bench; should have no more Incense offered 'em in the Churches; go cloath'd after the Spanish Fashion; should Assemble on Publick Affairs in a Chamber of the Vice-Roy's Palace; and have no longer any Jurisdiction on the Champian Country.

'Every one was seized with such Consternation, as if he had been Thunder-struck; but their Sorrow was much increased on the fifth of the same Month, when the Camp Master-General went to the Town-house, and seized all their Charters, and Original Copies of their Priviledges, and made 'em be burnt publickly by the Hands of the common Hang-man. The Prince de Condro was afterwards apprehended, to the great grief of his Family, but particularly the Princess Eleonora, his Sister, whose Tears were not shed alone: This Princess is not above Eighteen; her Beauty and Wit are miraculous, which astonish those about her.' Don Sancho's Eyes grew red

red at the remembrance of this Princefs, and I plainly perceiv'd Pity had not all the fhare in what he faid; yet he continued on his Difcourfe to me of Meffina.

'The Vice-Roy,' added he, 'publifht an Order, by which all the Citizens were enjoyn'd, under penalty of ten Years Imprifonment, and five thoufand Crowns Fine, to bring their Arms into his Palace. He at the fame time caus'd the great Bell in the Town-houfe to be taken down, and beaten to pieces in his fight: He ordered all the Bells in the Cathedral to be melted, to make a Statue of the King of Spain. And the Prince of Condro's Children were taken into Cuftody: But their Fear increafed, when the Vice-Roy ordered D. V. Zuffo's Head to be cut off. This Example of Severity Alarum'd all the People; and what appear'd moft terrible, was, That in the late Troubles, fome Families of Meffinois having with-

withdrawn themfelves into feveral Parts, the Marquefs de Liche, the Spanifh Embaffador at Rome, advifed them, as a Friend, to return into their own Country, affuring them all was Quiet, and that a General Pardon was already publifht; and for their greater affurance, gave them Pafports. Thefe poor People (who had not taken up Arms, and being not of the number of the Revolters, knowing their Innocency, could never have imagin'd they fhould have been treated as Criminals) return'd to Meffina; where they had fcarcely landed, but the Joy they had of feeing themfelves in their Native Country, and in the midft of their Friends, was fadly difturb'd, when they were feifed on, and the next Morning, without any Quarter, or regard to Sex or Age, by the Vice-Roy's Order, all hang'd. He afterwards fent to demolifh the great Tower of Palermo; and the principal Citizens of it, remonftrating againft the exceffive Impofitions positions on Corn, Silks, and other Commodities, the Marquefs de las Navas sent them all to the Gallies, without being moved by the Tears of their Wives, and the need so many poor Children might have of their Fathers.

'I must acknowledge,' continued Don Sancho, 'that my Nature is so averse to the Rigors every day exercis'd on these poor People, that I could not for all the World remain any longer at Messina. The Marquefs de las Navas was for sending to Madrid, to inform the King of what he had done. I intreated him to charge me with this Commission; and in effect he consented, and gave me his Letters, which I have delivered to the King at Madrid; and at the same time my Intercessions for the Prince de Condro: And I presume my good Offices will not be wholly useless to him.' 'I am perswaded,' said I to him, 'this was the principal Motive
of

of your Journey: I am no prying body, but methinks you are greatly concern'd for the Interefts of this Family.' 'It's true, Madam,' continued he, 'the Injuftice done this Unfortunate Prince does fenfibly affect me': 'Were he not Brother to the Princefs Eleonora,' faid I to him, 'perhaps you would not fo much lay it to heart. But no more of this; I perceive this Remembrance afflicts you. Pray let me rather hear from you what is moft remarkable in your Country.' 'Ah! Madam,' cried he, 'you infult over me; for you muft needs know, that Galicia is fo poor and mean a Countrey, that there's no place for bragging; not but that the Town of St. James de Compoftella is confiderable enough; it is the Capital of the Province, and fcarce one in Spain that's fuperiour to it in Riches and Greatnefs: Its Archbifhoprick is worth Seventy Thoufand Crowns a Year, and the Chapter has as much; It
ftands

ſtands in an agreeable Plain, ſurrounded with little Hills of moderate heighth; and it ſeems as if Nature had placed them there to defend the Town from thoſe deadly Blaſts which ariſe from other Mountains. Here is a Univerſity, fine Palaces, ſtately Churches, publick Places, and an Hoſpital, one of the moſt conſiderable, and beſt ſerv'd in Europe: It conſiſts of two Courts of extraordinary greatneſs, with Fountains in the midſt. Several Knights of St. James live in this Town; and the Metropolis, which is dedicated to this Saint, keeps his Body: It is extream ſtately, and prodigiouſly rich: It is pretended you hear a kind of Clattering at his Tomb, as if Arms were ſtruck one againſt another; and this noiſe is only heard when the Spaniards are to undergo any great Loſs. His Figure is repreſented on the Altar, and the Pilgrims thrice kiſs it, and put their Hats on his Head; for this is the chief part of the Ceremony:

mony: They have also another very singular one; they ascend the top of the Church, which is covered with great flat Stones; In this place stands a Cross of Iron, whereon the Pilgrims ever fasten some Rag, or Scrap of what they wear: They pass under this Cross by so strait a Passage that they are forced to crawl on their Bellies through it; and those who are not slender, are in danger of being bursten. And there have been some so ridiculous and superstitious, that having omitted to do this, they have expresly return'd back again three or four hundred Leagues; for you see here Pilgrims of all Nations. Here is a French Chappel, of which great Care is taken; It is said, the Kings of France have been always great Benefactors to it. The Church which is under ground is a better than that above; there are stately Tombs, and Epitaphs of great Antiquity, which exercise the Wits of Travellers. The Archiepiscopal Palace
is

is a vaſt Pile, and its Antiquity adds to its Beauty, inſtead of diminiſhing it. A Man of my Acquaintance, a great Searcher into Etymologies, aſſured me the Town of Compoſtella was ſo called, becauſe St. James was to ſuffer Martyrdom in the place where he ſhould ſee a Star appear at Compoſtella. It is true,' continued he, 'that ſome People pretend it to be thus; but the Peoples Credulity and Superſtition carries 'em further; for you are ſhew'd at Padron, near Compoſtella, an hollow Stone; and it is pretended this was the little Boat in which St. James arriv'd, after he had paſt ſo many Seas in it, which being of Stone, muſt have, without a ſignal Miracle, ſunk to the bottom.' 'I ſuppoſe,' ſaid I to him, 'you believe this to be moſt true.' He ſmiled, and continued his Diſcourſe: 'I cannot but give you the Deſcription of our Militia: They are called together every Year in the Month of October, and all the
Young

Young Men from the Age of Fifteen, are oblig'd to march; for fhould it happen that a Father, or any other Relation fhould conceal his Son or Kinfman, and thofe who are Officers fhould come to know it, they would condemn him who has fo offended, to perpetual Imprifonment. There have been fome Examples of this, but they are rare; for the Peafants are fo infinitely pleas'd to fee themfelves Arm'd and treated as Cavalieros & de Nobles Soldados del Rey, that they would not for any Confideration be wanting to fhew themfelves on this occafion. You fhall feldom fee in an whole Regiment any Souldier that has more Shirts than that on his Back; and the Stuff they wear, feems for its Coarfenefs to be made of Pack-thread: their Shooes are made of Cord; they wear no Stockings, yet every Man has his Peacock, or Dunghil-Cock's Feather in his Cap, which is tied up behind, with a Rag about his Neck in form of

a

a Ruff; their Sword oftentimes hangs by their fide tied with a bit of Cord, and ordinary without a Scabbard; the reſt of their Arms is feldom in better Order: And in this Equipage they march gravely to Tuy, where is the General Rendezvouz, it being a Frontier place to Portugal. There are three which lie thus, the above-mention'd, Cindud-Rodrigo, and Badajoz, but Tuy is the beſt guarded, becauſe it is over-againſt Valentia, a confiderable Town belonging to the King of Portugal, and which has been carefully fortifi'd: Theſe two Towns are ſo near, that their Cannon will reach each other; and if the Portugaiſes have omitted nothing to put Valentia out of danger of being inſulted over, the Spaniards pretend Tuy is in as good a Condition to defend it felf; It ſtands on an Hill, whoſe lower part is waſh'd by the River Minhio; it has good Ramparts, ſtrong Walls, and good ſtore of Artillery. It is here, I ſay, fay, where thefe our Champions bid Defiance to the King's Enemies, and in a ftrutting Bravery, declare, they do not fear 'em. Perhaps fomething of this may happen in time, for here are form'd as good Troops as in any other part of Spain. However, this is a great lofs to the Kingdom, the whole Youth being thus taken up; for the Lands, for the moft part lye untill'd, and on the fide of St. James de Compoftella, you wou'd think you faw a Wildernefs; on that of the Ocean, the Country being better and more peopled, yields greater Profit, and all things neceffary and convenient, as Oranges, Lemmons, and Pomgranates, feveral forts of Fruits, and excellent Fifh, efpecially Pilchards, more delicate than thofe which came from Royan to Bordeaux.

' One of the moft remarkable things, in my mind, in this Kingdom, is the Town of Doienfe, one part of which always enjoys the Sweetnefs of the
Spring,

Spring, and the Fruits of Autumn, by reaſon of ſeveral Springs of boiling Water, which warm the Air by their Exhalations; whil'ſt the other part of this ſame Town ſuffers the Rigors of the longeſt Winters, ſtanding as it does at the Foot of a very cold Mountain; ſo that you find in the ſpace of one only Seaſon, all thoſe which compoſe the courſe of the Year.'

'You ſay nothing,' replied I to him, 'of the marvellous Fountain, call'd Louzano.' 'Who have told you of it, Madam?' anſwer'd he. 'Perſons that have ſeen it,' added I. 'You have been then told,' continu'd he, 'that on the top of the Mountain of Cerbret, you find this Fountain at the Source of the River Lours; which has Flux and Reflux as the Sea, tho' it be at twenty Leagues diſtance from it; that the greater the Heats are, the more Water it caſts, that this Water is ſometimes cold as Ice, and ſometimes as hot as if it boil'd, there being
no

no Natural Cause to be giv'n for it.' 'You learn me Particulars I was ignorant of,' said I to him, 'and this is doing me a great Pleasure, for I want not for Curiosity in relation to things uncommon.' 'I wish,' replied he, ''twas not so late, I would give you an account of several Rarities in Spain, and which perhaps you would gladly learn.' 'I leave you for to Night,' said I to him, 'but I hope before we come to Madrid, we shall have an opportunity of discoursing of them.' He very civilly made me a Promise; and the Play being ended, we bad one another good night.

When I would go to rest, I was led into a Gallery full of Beds, as you see in Hospitals: I said, this was ridiculous; and that needing only four, what occasion was there for shewing me forty, and to put me into such an open place to starve me? I was answer'd, This was the best place in the House, and I must take up with it.

it. I caus'd my Bed to be made, when scarce was I laid down, but some body knockt softly at my Door; my Women opened it, and remained much surpriz'd to see the Master and Mistress followed by a dozen of sorry creatures, and so cloath'd that they were half naked. I drew my Curtain at the Noise they made, and opened more mine Eyes at the sight of this Noble Company. The Mistress drew near to me, and told me, These were honest Travellers, who were coming into the Beds which remained empty. 'How, lie here?' said I, 'I believe you have lost your Senses.' 'I should have lost 'em indeed,' replied she, 'should I let so many Beds stand Empty. Either, Madam, you must pay for them, or these honest Gentlemen must lye in them.' I cannot express my Rage to you; I was in the mind to send for Don Fernand and my Knights, who would have sooner made 'em pass through the Win-

Windows than through the Doors: But I confidered this could not be done without fome Difturbance, and therefore I came to Terms, and agreed to pay 20 *d*. for each Bed; they are hardly dearer at Fontainbleau when the Court is there. Thefe Illuftrious Dons, or, to fpeak better, Tatterdemalions, who had the Infolence to come into my Room, immediately withdrew, having made me feveral profound Reverences.

The next Morning I thought to have burft with laughter, tho' twas at my Coft, when I difcovered mine Hoftefs's Trick to ruin me: For you muft know in the firft place, that thefe pretended Travellers were their Neighbours, and that they are accuftomed to this Stratagem, when they fee Strangers: But when I would have reckoned the Beds to pay for 'em, they were rowled all of 'em into the midft of the Gallery; there were divers wretched Troughs of Straw pull'd out, which were

were hardly good enough to entertain Dogs, yet I muſt pay for each 20 *d*. Four Piſtoles ended our Diſpute. I was not able to put my ſelf in a Paſſion, ſuch ſingularity did I find in this Management. I would not recount this little Accident to you, did it not ſerve to give you ſome inſight into the Humour of this Nation.

We ſet out from Burgos very late, the Weather was ſo bad, and there had fall'n in the Night ſuch great quantity of Rain, that I tarry'd there as long as I could, in expectation of its ceaſing. In fine, I came to a Reſolution, and aſcended my Litter. I had not gotten far from the Town, but I repented of my leaving it; no Track cou'd be ſeen, eſpecially on a very high ſteep Mountain, over which we muſt neceſſarily paſs. One of our Mule-drivers, who went before, ſtruck too far on the Edge of this Mountain, ſo that he fell with his Mule into a kind of Precipice, where he broke his Head,

Head, and put his Arm out of joynt; this being the famous Philip de St. Sebaftian, the moft intelligent of all his Profeffion, and who commonly carries Perfons of Quality to Madrid; he was therefore much bemoaned; and we remain'd a great while before we could hale him out from the fcurvy place where he had fall'n; Don Fernand was fo compaffionate as to let him have his Litter. The Night came fpeedily on us, and we could have comforted our felves, could we have return'd to Burgos, but it was impoffible, the Ways were no lefs covered with Snow on that fide, than all the reft; fo that we put in at Madrigalefco, which has not above a dozen Houfes, and I may fay we were befieg'd without having any Enemies. This Adventure gave us fome difturbance, tho' we had brought Provifions with us for feveral Days. The beft Houfe of the Town was half uncovered; and I was fcarce lodged there, when a vener-

venerable Old Man askt for me on the part of a Lady who was juſt arriv'd: He made me a Compliment, and told me, He was inform'd this was the only place where there was any tolerable Entertainment; and therefore intreated me to ſpare her ſome room. He added, She was a Perſon of Quality of Andalouſia, was lately a Widow, and that he had the Honour to belong to her.

One of our Knights, named Don Eſteve de Carjaval, who is of the ſame Country, fail'd not to demand her Name of the old Gentleman: He told him, ſhe was the Marchioneſs de Los Rios. At this Name he turn'd towards me, and ſpake to me of her as of a Perſon whoſe Merit and Fortune were very conſiderable: I readily accepted of this good Company; She immediately came in her Litter, out of which ſhe had not deſcended, having found no Houſe where ſhe could abide.

Her Dreſs ſeem'd to me very ſingular;

lar; had she not been so handsome as she was, she could never have appear'd in any sort tolerable: Her Gown and Petticoat was of black Serge, and over them a kind of Linnen Surplice, which reacht down lower than her Knees; the Sleeves were long, and strait in the Arm, which hung over her Hands: This Surplice was fastned to her gown, and being not pleated behind, it seem'd like a Bib: She wore on her Head a piece of Muslin, which covered her Face, and one would have taken it for a Religiose's Hood; this covered her Neck, and reach'd down very low: There appear'd no Hair on her Head, they were all hid under this Muslin: She wore a great Mantle of black Taffaty, which covered her Heels; and over this Mantle she had an Hat, whose Brims were very large, fastned under her Chin with silken Twist. I was told they wear this but only when they travel.

This

This is the Habit of the Widows and Duenna's, a Drefs which is infupportable to my fight; and fhould one meet with a Woman in the Night thus cloath'd, one might be ftartled without Reproach; yet the Lady was very beautiful in this Unfeemly Drefs. They never leave it, unlefs they marry; and they are oblig'd to bewail the Death of an Husband, whom they could not endure when living.

I was inform'd they pafs the firft Year of their Mourning in a Chamber hung with Black, wherein there is not the leaft glimmering of Day-light to be feen; they fit crofs-legg'd on a little Holland-Quilt. When this Year is ended, they retire into a Chamber hung with Gray: they muft have no Pictures, nor Looking-Glaffes, nor Cabinets, nor fine Tables, nor Plate, neither muft they have any Diamonds, or wear any Colours: However modeft they are, they muft live fo retired, that it muft feem their Soul is already
in

in the other World. This Conſtrant is the cauſe that ſeveral Ladies who are wealthy, and eſpecially in rich Houſhold-Goods, marry again to have the ſatisfaction of making uſe of them.

After the firſt Compliments, I inform'd my ſelf from this mournful Widow where ſhe was going; ſhe told me, She had not for a long time ſeen a Friend of her Mother's who was a Religious at Laſhuelgas de Burgos, which is a famous Nunnery, wherein there is an hundred and fifty Nuns, moſt of 'em the Daughters of Princes, Dukes, and Titulado's. She added, That the Abbeſs is Lady of fourteen large Towns, and above fifty other Places wherein ſhe chuſes Governors and Magiſtrates; that ſhe is Superior of ſeventeen Convents; Collates to ſeveral Benefices, and diſpoſes of twelve Commanderſhips in favour of whom ſhe pleaſes. She told me ſhe deſign'd to paſs ſome time in this Monaſtery: 'Can you, Madam,' ſaid I to

to her, 'accuftom yourfelf to fo retired a Life as is that of a Convent?' 'It will be no hard matter,' faid fhe, 'for I believe I fee fewer People at my own Houfe than I fhall fee there; and in effect thefe Religious have Liberty enough: They are commonly the handfomeft young Women of the Family who are there; thefe enter therein fo young, that they know not what they are made to leave, nor what they undertake at the Age of fix or feven, and it may be fooner. They are caufed to make Vows, when 'tis often the Father or Mother, or fome near Relation, who pronounce them for 'em, whilft the little Sacrifice difports herfelf with Sugar-plums, and lets 'em drefs her how they will: Yet the Bargain holds, there's no unfaying it; however, they have every thing which can be expected in their Condition. There are at Madrid fome whom they call the Ladies of St. James: they are properly Canonneffes,
who

who make their Tryals like the Knights of this Order; they bear, like them, a Sword, made in form of a Cross, embroidered with Crimson Silk; they have 'em on their Scapularies and great Cloaks, which are white: These Ladies House is very stately; all who come to visit 'em enter without any difficulty; their Apartments are very fine, and every whit as well furnisht as if they were at large in the World; they enjoy great Pensions, and each of 'em has three or four Women to wait on them: It's true, they never stir out, nor see their nearest Relations, but through several Grates. This perhaps would look horrid in another Country, but in Spain they are accustom'd to Confinement.

' There are Convents where the Religious see more Cavaliers than the Women who live at large, neither are they less gallant: It is impossible for any to have more Gayety than they;
and,

and, as I have already told you, Madam, here are more Beauties than abroad; but it muſt be granted, there are ſeveral among them who are deeply ſenſible at their having been ſo ſoon ſacrific'd; they think of the Pleaſures which they have never taſted, as the only ones which can make this Life Happy. They paſs theirs in a Condition worthy of Compaſſion, always telling you, they are there by Force; and that the Vows they are made to repeat at the Age of five or ſix Years, are to be regarded like Childrens Plays.'

'Madam,' ſaid I to her, 'it wou'd have been great pity, had your Relations deſign'd you for ſuch a Life; and one may judge, in beholding you, that all the beautiful Spaniſh Ladies are not Religioſes.' 'Alas, Madam,' ſaid ſhe, in fetching a deep Sigh, 'I know not what I wou'd be; it ſeems I am of a very odd Humor, not to be contented with my Fortune: but one has ſometimes Uneaſineſſes which are unac-

unaccountable to Reason.' In ending these words, she fastned her Eyes to the ground, and fell into such a deep fit of Musing, that I cou'd easily perceive something disturb'd her.

Whatever Curiosity I had to know the Subject, we had been so little together, that I dared not desire to be her Confident; but to draw her from the melancholy Posture she was in, I entreated her to tell me some News of the Court of Spain, seeing she came from Madrid. She did what she cou'd to recover herself: she then told me, There were great shews of Joy at Court on the Queen's Birth-day: that the King had sent one of the Gentlemen of his Chamber to Toledo, to Compliment her from him: Yet these fine Appearances hindred not the Marquess de Mansera, the Queen's Major Domo, from receiving Orders to retire twenty Leagues from the Court, which had greatly mortifi'd this Princess. She inform'd us, That the Fleet which

which carried Troops to Galicia, was unhappily caſt away on the Coaſts of Portugal. That the little Dutcheſs de Terra Nova, was to Eſpouſe Don Nicolo Pignatelli, Prince de Monteleon, her Uncle. That the Marqueſs de Leganez had refuſed the Vice-royalty of Sardagnia, being in love with a fine Lady, whom he cou'd not find in his heart to leave. That Don Carlos de Omodei, Marqueſs d' Almonazid, was dangerouſly ill, at his Diſappointment of being admitted a Grandee of Spain, to which he pretended, having marry'd the Heireſs of the Houſe and Grandeurſhip of Caſtel Rodrigue; and that which moſt ſenſibly afflicted him, was, that Don Ariel de Guſman, this Lady's firſt Husband, had enjoyed this Honour; ſo that he cou'd not but look on the Difficulties thrown in his way as a ſlighting of his Perſon: 'In truth, Madam,' ſaid I to her, 'I can hardly comprehend how a Man of ſence, can with ſuch eagerneſs purſue, and be ſo greatly

greatly dejected at a Disappointment of this Nature.' 'We are otherwise affected in Spain,' replied the beautiful Widow, 'and this Instance is a proof of it.'

Don Frederic de Cardonne, who greatly interested himself for the Duke de Medina Celi, askt her News of him: 'The King,' said she, 'has lately made him President of the Indies. The Queen-Mother has wrote to the King, on the Report which runs, that he is about Marrying; that she is surpriz'd things are already gone so far, and he has not acquainted her with them. She adds in her Letter, She advised him in the mean time, whilst all things were ready for this Ceremony, to make a Journey to Catalonia and Arragon. Don John of Austria sufficiently understands the Necessity of this, and he presses the King to depart, to content these People, in promising by Oath, according as is customary to new Kings, to maintain all

all their ancient Priviledges.' 'Have then, Madam,' ſaid I to her, interrupting her, 'the Arrogonois any other Priviledges than the Caſtillans?' 'Very particular ones,' replied ſhe, 'and you being a Stranger, I believe you will be willing to let me inform you of them.' Here's what I learnt:

The Daughter of Count Julien, named Cava, was one of the moſt beautiful Ladies in the World: King Rodrigue became ſo paſſionately in love with her, that his Affection knowing no Bounds, tranſported him beyond all meaſure. The Father, who was then in Affrica, inform'd of the Outrage done his Daughter, who breath'd nothing but Revenge, treated with the Moors, and ſupplied 'em with the means to enter into Spain,* and to make there, for ſundry Ages, all

* This happened in 714, after the Battle of St. Martin, wherein D. Rodrigue loſt his Life; others ſay, he fled into Portugal, and died in a Town there call'd Viſcii.

all thofe Ravages fet forth at large in Hiftory.

The Arragonois were the firft who fhook off the Yoak of thefe Barbarians; and finding no more among them any Princes of the Race of Gothifh Kings, they agreed to Elect one, and caft their eyes on a Lord of the Country, call'd Garci Ximinex; but they being Mafters, to impofe Laws on him, and finding himfelf fufficiently Happy that he might Rule over them under any Condition, thefe People therefore confined him within narrow Bounds.

They agreed, That as foon as their Monarch fhou'd break through any of their Laws, he fhou'd immediately forfeit his Power, and they be at full liberty to chufe another, though he were a Pagan: and to hinder him from violating their Priviledges, and to defend themfelves againft him, they eftablifht a Soveraign Magiftrate, whom they call'd the Jufticia, whofe
Office

Office was to obferve the Conduct of the King, the Judges, and the People: but the Power of a Soveraign being likely to Awe a meer Particular, to Affure the Jufticia in the Execution of his Office, they ordered, That he might not fuffer either in his Perfon or Goods, but by a compleat Affembly of the States, which they call Las Cortes.

They moreover provided, That if the King fhou'd Opprefs any one of his Subjects, the great and confiderable Men of the Kingdom might affemble themfelves, and hinder his receiving any of his Revenues, till the Innocent was acquitted, and re-eftablifht in his former Rights. And to make Garci Ximinez timely fenfible of the Power this Man had over him, they fet him on a kind of a Throne, and made the King to kneel down bare headed before him, to receive from him his Oath of keeping their Priviledges. This Ceremony ended, they

they acknowledge him their Soveraign, but in as odd as difrespectful a Manner, for inftead of promifing him Fidelity and Obedience, they fay to him, 'We who are as good Men as yourfelf, we make you our King and Governour, on Condition you keep to us our Rights and Properties, otherwife we Difacknowledge you.'

The King, Don Pedro, in procefs of time coming to the Crown, rellifht this Cuftom, as unworthy of the Regal State; and it fo greatly difgufted him, that by his Authority and Intreaties, and the Offers he made of beftowing feveral notable Priviledges on the Kingdom, he procured the Abolifhment of this, in an Affembly of the States: he got this general Confent in Writing, which was prefented to him. As foon as he had the Parchment, he drew out his Dagger, and pierced his Hand with it, faying, ' 'Twas fit a Law which gave Subjects the Liberty of chufing their
Sov-

Soveraign, should be Efaced with their Sovereign's Bloud.' His Statue is still seen in the Deputation-hall of Saragossa: he holds a Dagger in one Hand, and the Charter in the other. The late Kings have not been such Religious Observers of their Priviledges as the first.

But there is a Law still in force, and which is very singular, and this they call, 'The Law of Manifestation'; which is, That if an Arragonois had Wrong done him in Judgment, in consigning 500 Crowns, he may bring his Cause before the Justicia, who is obliged, after an exact Perquisition, to punish him who has giv'n a wrong Sentence: And if he fails therein, the oppreft Person may have Recourse to the States of the Kingdom, who Assemble and Nominate five Persons of their Body, which is to say, of the Prime Nobility, the Ecclesiasticks, the Gentry and Commonalty: they appoint three out of the first Rank, and two

two from each of the others. But it is obfervable, they choofe the moft Ignorant to Judge the moft able Men in the Gown, whether to Difgrace 'em the more for their Fault, or, as they alledge, 'That Juftice fhould be fo clear, that the very Plow-men, and thofe who underftand the leaft, fhould difcern it without the help of Oratory.' It is likewife affirm'd, That the Judges tremble when they pronounce a Sentence, fearing left it turn againft themfelves, to the lofs of their Lives or Eftates, fhould they commit the leaft Fault therein, either wilfully, or through Inadvertency. It were well if this Cuftom were obferved in all Kingdoms: but this is rather to be wifh'd than expected.

Yet what is no lefs fingular, is, That Juftice remains always Soveraign; and though the Unjuft Judge be punifh'd feverely for his wrong Decree, yet it fubfifts in its full force, and is fully executed: If then any Unhappy

happy Wretch be fentenced to Death, he is not fpared, tho' his Innocency be difcovered, and made as clear as Noon-day; but his Judges are executed too before his Face; which, in my mind, is a poor Confolation. If the Judge accufed, has juftly perform'd his Office, the Plaintiff leaves the 500 Crowns which he had confign'd: But were he to lofe an 100000 Crowns of Annual Revenue, by the Sentence he complains of, the Sentence or Decree remains good, and the Judge is only condemn'd to pay him likewife 500 Crowns; the reft of this Judge's Eftate is forfeited to the King: which is, in my Opinion, another Point of Injuftice; for in fine, he ought, above all others, to have Recompenfe made him who fuffers by a wrong Sentence.

Thefe fame People have another Cuftom, to diftinguifh by the Punifhment the Crime committed: for Example, A Cavalier, who has kill'd another in Duel (for they are here ftrictly strictly forbid), he has his Head cut off before; and he that has Assassinated, his is cut off behind. This is to distinguish him who has behaved himself like a brave Man, from him that kills you Treacherously.

She added, That to speak in general of the Arragonois, They have a Natural Pride, which is hard to be suppress'd: but likewise to do them Justice, there are people of brave Minds to be found among them; insomuch, that they are easily discern'd from all the rest of the King of Spain's Subjects: That they have never wanted Great Men, from their first King to Ferdinand: That they counted such a great number of them, as would scarce be believ'd: However, they have greatly recommended themselves by their Valour and Conduct. That as to the rest, their Country was so little fruitful, that excepting some Valleys which were watered by Channels, whose Water came from

the

the Ebre, the reſt was ſo dry and ſandy, that you meet with ſcarce any thing elſe but ſtony and parched up places: That Sarragoſſa is a great City, the Houſes finer than at Madrid; the Publick Places adorn'd with Arches; that the Holy Street, where the Courſes are run, is ſo long and large, as may make it paſs for a great and vaſt place, having ſeveral great Mens Palaces on it; that of Caſtelmorato being one of the pleaſanteſt: That the Vault of St. Francis's Church was very curious, for being of extraordinary Largeneſs, yet 'tis upheld by no Pillars: That the City is not ſtrong, but the Inhabitants ſo ſtout, that it needed no Walls; that it has never a Fountain, this being one of its greateſt Defects: That the Ebre carried no Boats, the River being full of dangerous Rocks. As to the reſt, the Archbiſhoprick was worth 60000 Crowns a year: That the Vice-Royalty brought in no Revenue, being a Place of Honour,

nour, fit only for great Lords to bear the Expence of it, to maintain their Rank, and keep the People under, who are Naturally Fierce and Imperious, not Affable to Strangers; and so little desirous of making Acquaintance, that they chuse rather to stay at Home alone all their Life-time, than stir out to procure Friendships: That here is a severe Inquisition, who have a stately Palace, and a most Rigid Court of Justice; Yet this does not hinder great Troops of Robbers, call'd Bandoleros, from Ravaging, and dispersing themselves over all Spain; who give no Quarter to Travellers, snatching up sometimes Women of Quality, whom they afterwards set at Ransom, for their Parents to Redeem; but when they are Handsome they keep them: And this is the greatest Misfortune can happen to 'em, being forced to spend their Days with the Worst of Men, who keep them in dreadful Caves, or carry them along with them

on

on Horse-back, being so furiously jealous of 'em, that one of their Captains (having been lately set upon by Souldiers sent into the Mountains to seize on him) being mortally wounded, and having his Mistress with him, who was of the Marquess de Camaraza, a Grandee of Spain's Family; When she saw him in this Condition, she thought only of making Use of this favourable Opportunity of saving her self; which he perceiving, dying, as he was, he catch'd hold of her Hair, and struck his Dagger into her Breast, Being not willing, said he, that another should possess a Treasure which had been so dear to him. And this is what himself acknowledg'd to the Souldiers who found him, and saw this sad Spectacle.

The Beautiful Marchioness here held her peace; and I return'd her all due Thanks for the Favour she did me, in informing me of these Curiosities; and of which, perhaps without her, I might

might have been Ignorant all my Life. 'I do not think, Madam,' said she to me, ' you owe me such Thanks; I rather fear the having deserved Reproaches for so long and tiresome a Conversation.'

I would not let her leave me to eat elsewhere; and I obliged her to lye with me, she having no Bed. So Civil and Courteous a Proceeding made her much my Friend: She assured me of this in such Affectionate Terms, that I could not doubt of it; for I must tell you, the Spanish Women are more Caressing than we, and are far more Kind and Tender to those they profess Friendship. In fine, I could not forbear telling her, 'That if she had all the Kindness for me she made profession, she must be so complaisant, to inform me, What made her seem so melancholly? That I had heard her fetch deep Sighs in the Night, and appear'd very Restless and Disconsolate; That if she could find any

any Comfort in sharing her Grief with me, I offered my Service to her, as a most faithful Friend.' She embraced me with great Affection, and told me without delay, she would immediately satisfie my Curiosity; which she did in these Terms:

'Seeing you are desirous to know me, I must without disguising to you any thing, acknowledge my Weaknesses to you; and by my Sincerity and Open-heartedness, deserve a Curiosity as obliging as yours:

'I come not of such a Family as may claim Nobility; my Father's Name was Davila; he was only a Banker, but he was in good Credit, and was moderately Wealthy: We are of Seville, Capital of Andalousia, and we have ever dwelt there. My Mother knew the World, she saw many People of Quality, and having no Children but me, she took great care of my Education: It did not appear ill-bestowed on me; for I had
the

the good Fortune to get the good Will of moſt that ſaw me.

'We had two Neighbours who came often to our Houſe, who were very welcome both to my Father and Mother: Their Condition and Age were in no ſort alike; One was the Marqueſs de Los Rios, a Perſon Wealthy and Noble; he was a Widower, and well advanced in years: the other was the Son of a great Merchant, who traded to the Indies; he was Young and Handſome, he had Wit, and a very graceful Behaviour; his Name was Mendez: He was not long before he fell paſſionately in Love with me; ſo that he omitted nothing which might pleaſe me, and gain my Affections.

'He was in all places where he knew I was to paſs; he ſpent whole Nights under my Windows, to ſing Verſes which he had compoſed and ſet to my Praiſe, which he had very well accompany'd with his Harp.

'But

'But seeing his Attendancies had not all the Effect he expected, and having past some time in this manner, without daring to mention his Affection to me, he at length resolv'd to make use of the first occasion to acquaint me with it. I avoided him ever since I had a Conversation with one of my Friends, who had more Experience and Knowledge of the World than I: I had felt, that Mendez's Company gave me Joy, and that my Heart had an Emotion for him, which it had not for others: That when his Affairs, or our Visits hindred him from seeing me, I grew restless; and loving this young Woman, above others, and being as dear to her, she observ'd I was not so free and gay as I was wont, and that my Eyes were sometimes attentively fixed on Mendez. One Day when she rally'd with me about it, I said to her very innocently, "My dear Henrietta, define to me the Sentiments I have for Mendez: I know not

not whether I ought to be afraid of them, and whether I ought not to defend my felf from them. I feel I know not what fort of Trouble and Pleafure arifing in my Breaft." She began to laugh, fhe embraced me, and faid to me, "My dear Heart, you are in Love." "Who, I in Love?" reply'd I, in amaze: "You joke with me; I neither am, nor will be in Love." "This depends not always on us," continued fhe, with a more ferious Air, "our Stars decide this before our Hearts. But in earneft, what is it fo much ftartles you? Mendez is in a Condition equal to yours; he deferves well, a good comely Man; and if his Affairs go on with the fame Succefs as they have done hitherto, you may live very happily with him." "And whence fhould I learn," reply'd I, interrupting her, "that he will be happy with me, and that he fo much as thinks this?" "O, take my Word for it," anfwer'd fhe, "whatever he has

has done has its Defigns; for Men are not wont to pafs Nights under Windows, and the Days in following a Perfon for whom they have nothing but Indifferency."

'After fome other Difcourfe of this Nature, fhe left me, and I refolv'd, maugre the Repugnance I felt in me, to give Mendez no opportunity of fpeaking to me in particular.

'But one Night as I was walking in the Garden, he came towards me: I was perplext to fee my felf alone with him; and he had the opportunity of obferving it on my Countenance, and in the manner after which I receiv'd him. This could not divert him from the defign he had of entertaining me: "How Happy am I Madam," faid he, "to find you alone? But do I call my felf Happy! Perhaps I know not what I fay: for it may be you will not receive a Secret with which I would entruft you." "I am as yet fo young," faid I to him, blufhing, "that

"that I would advife you to fay nothing to me, unlefs you would have me impart it to my Companions." "Alas," continued he, "fhould I tell you, I Adore you; that all my Happinefs depends on the Inclinations you have towards me: That I cannot live without fome Certainty, that I may one day pleafe you; will you tell this to your Companions?" "No," faid I to him, in great perplexity, "I would look on this Confidence as a Railery; and not believing it my felf, I would not hazard its being left to be believ'd by others."

'We were interrupted as I ended thefe words; and he appear'd to me not over-content with the Anfwer I made him; and a while after he found an opportunity to reproach me with it.

'I could not but give a favourable Ear to the Inclinations I had towards him; every thing he told me feem'd to me to have its particular Gracefulnefs:

nefs: And it was no hard matter for him to perfwade me, that he lov'd me above all things in the World.

'In the mean time, the Marquefs de Los Rios took fuch a liking to me, and my Perfon and Behaviour ran fo deeply in his Thoughts, that he wholly applied himfelf to pleafe me. He was very nice and cautious; he could not refolve with himfelf to owe me wholly to my Parents authority: He well knew they would receive as an Honour the Intentions he had for me; but he was for gaining my Confent before he demanded theirs.

'In this Defign he faid all to me he thought was like to take with me. I anfwer'd him I fhould always think it an indifpenfable Duty to obey my Father: yet our Ages were fo different, that I told him, I thought 'twere better he left off thinking of me; that I fhould have an everlafting Acknowledgment for the advantageous Intentions he had for me; and therefore I would

would esteem him, tho I could not love him. Having heard what I said, he was some time without speaking, and immediately taking up a very generous Resolution: "Lovely Mariana," says he, "you might have made me the happiest Man in the World; and if you were ambitious, I had wherewith to satisfie you: But you refuse me, and I desire to be anothers: I consent to it; I love you too well to be in suspence, whether you are to be satisfied or I; I therefore wholly sacrifice my Happiness to you, and leave you for ever." In ending these Words he left me, and appear'd so afflicted, that I could not forbear being concern'd.

'Mendez arriv'd a while after, and found me melancholly: He was so earnest with me to know the Cause, that I could not deny him this Proof of my Complaisance. Any one but he would have had a sensible Obligation at the Exclusion I came from giving his Rival: But far from seeming to value

value it, he told me, He saw in mine Eyes the Regret I had for a Lover, who could place me in another sort of a Rank than he was able; and that my Proceeding was very Cruel. In vain [I] endeavoured to make him sensible of the Injustice of this; but all I could say, could not hinder him from charging me with Inconstancy. I remain'd vext, and surpriz'd at this his Way of Dealing, and was several days without speaking to him.

'He, in fine, at last understood he had no Reason to Complain; he came to me, and begg'd my Pardon, and testified to me a great Displeasure at his own Jealousie: He excused himself, as all Lovers do, on the strength of his Passion. I had so much Weakness as to be willing to forget the Trouble he had given me: we made up the Matter between us, and he continued on his Courtship.

'His Father having understood the Passion he had for me, thought he could

could not procure him a more advantageous Marriage: he took notice of it to him, and came afterwards to my Father, to open to him the Propofal: they had been long Friends; he was favourably heard, and they eafily agreed on the Matter.

'Mendez came to inform me of the News, with fuch Tranfports as would have feem'd ridiculous to any other than a Miftrefs. My Mother order'd me to look kindly on him, telling me, this Affair would be advantageous to me: and as foon as the India-Fleet fhould arrive, wherein he was greatly concern'd, the Marriage fhould be concluded.

'Whilft matters thus paft, the Marquefs de Los Rios had retired to one of his Country-Houfes, where he fcarcely faw any one: He led a languifhing Life; he ftill lov'd me, but hindred himfelf from telling me fo, and from comforting himfelf by this innocent Remedy.

'In

'In fine, his Body could not refift the Heavinefs of his Mind; he fell dangeroufly ill, and being told by the Phyficians, there was no hope of his Recovery, he pluckt up his Spirits to write me the moft affectionate Letter imaginable, and fent at the fame time to me a Deed of Gift of all his Eftate, in cafe he dyed. My Mother was in my Chamber, when a Gentleman prefented this Packet from him; fhe would know what it contain'd.

'I could not forbear at the fame time, telling her what had paft; and we were both of us in the greateft furprize at the Marquefs's extream Generofity. She fent him word, that I fhould go with my Family to thank him for a Liberality which I had no ways deferv'd: And in particular, fhe fharply reprehended me for having made a Myftery of a thing to her with which I ought to have immediately acquainted her. I threw myfelf at her Feet; I excufed myfelf the beft I could,

could, and testifi'd such great Sorrow for having displeas'd her, that she easily pardon'd me. Leaving my Chamber, she went to my Father, and having learnt him all which had past, they resolv'd to go the next Morning to see the Marquess, and to carry me with them.

'I acquainted Mendez with this in the Evening; and the Fear I had, lest my Parents should, in fine, make me marry this old Man, if he chanced to escape out of his Sickness. However sensible I appear'd to him of this, he was so far transported, and reproacht me so greatly with it, that I must have lov'd him as much as I did, not to have broke off with him: But he had such an Ascendant over me, that though he was the Injustest of all Men, yet I thought him the most Reasonable.

'We were at the Marquess de Los Rios's; his Country-house was not above two Leagues from Seville: Dying, as he was, he receiv'd us with such

such Joy as was easily observable. My Father testifi'd to him his Grief, to see him in so low a Condition, thankt him for the Donation he made me, and assured him, If he could find a fair and just Pretence, he would break off with Mendez, to whom he had engaged his Word: That should this happen, he promist him solemnly I should be no Body's but his. He receiv'd this Assurance in the same manner as if he had receiv'd his perfect Felicity; but he knew well the Dolor I conceiv'd thereat: I became Pale, my Eyes were covered with Tears; and when we were about leaving him, he desired me to draw near to him; he told me with a languishing Tone: "Fear nothing, Mariana; I love you too well to displease you; you shall have Mendez, seeing your Affections are engaged to him." I answer'd him: "I had no particular Inclination for him; but being commanded to respect him, as a Man who
was

was to be my Husband, I could do no otherwife; however, I intreated him to be well."

'This feem'd to me the leaft ftep I could take towards a Perfon to whom I had fo great Obligations. He appear'd thereat fufficiently fatisfy'd, attempting to take my Hand and kifs it: "Remember," faid he to me, "you enjoyn me to live; and that my Life being your Work, you will be oblig'd to conferve it." We return'd at Night, and the Impatient Mendez waited for us, to make me new Reproaches: I took 'em as I was wont, as Proofs of his Paffion: and having juftified my felf, I askt him, What News there was of the Fleet? "Alas!" faid he to me, "my Father has receiv'd fuch as drives me to Defpair: I dare not inform you." "Have you any thing feparate from me?" faid I to him, looking tenderly on him: "Would you have me to be as referv'd to you?" "I am too Happy," replied he, "in that you have

have fuch favourable Difpofitions; and being not able to keep any Secret from you, I muft plainly tell you, That the Galion in which is our whole Eftate, is fplit and loft, running againft a Rock. But I fhould be lefs fenfible, how greatly foever I am Intereft, did I not look on the Unhappy Confequences of this Lofs: Your Prefence will reftore the Marquefs de Los Rios to his Health; his Sentiments for you are known in your Family; he is Rich, and a great Lord: I become Miferable; and if you forfake me, my dear Mariana, I fhall have no more Hope but in a fpeedy Death." I was pierced with Sorrow at this fad News: I took one of his Hands, and clofing it with mine, I faid to him, "My dear Mendez, do not think me capable of loving you, and yet leaving you, by the Effects of your good or bad Fortune: if you be able to bear up againft it, believe me fo too. I call Heaven to witnefs," continued I, " provided you love

love me, and be faithful to me, that I will never forsake you; and let it punish me if ever I prove Inconstant."

'He testified all the Acknowedgements he ought me for such affectionate Assurances, and we resolved not to divulge this Accident.

'I withdrew very melancholly, and shut my self up in my Closet, ruminating on the Consequences of this sad Disaster. I was still there, when I heard some Body knocking softly at the Shutters of my Window: I drew near, and saw Mendez by the Light of the Moon: "What do you here," said I to him, "at this time of the Night?" "Alas," answer'd he to me, "I was trying whether I could speak with you before I departed: My Father has again lately received News of the Galion, and will have me immediately go where she is run aground, to endeavour to save something: It is a great way thither, and I shall be a great while without seeing you.

you. Ah, dear Mariana, during all this time will you be as good as your Word to me? May I hope my dear Miſtreſs will be faithful to me?" "What Reaſon have I given you, Mendez," ſaid I, interrupting him, "to doubt it? Yes," continued I, "I will love you were you the moſt Unfortunate Man in the World."

'It would be to abuſe your Patience, Madam, to relate to you whatever we ſaid in this doleful Separation; and though there appear'd no Danger, yet our Hearts had a foreboding of what was afterwards to happen to us. The Day began to appear, and we muſt bid Adieu: I ſaw him ſhed Tears, which were accompanied with mine.

'I threw myſelf on my Bed, rowling a thouſand ſad Thoughts in my Mind; and I appear'd the next Morning ſo out of Order, that my Father and Mother were afraid I was falling into ſome dangerous fit of Sickneſs.

'Mendez his Father came to make
them

them a Viſit, to excuſe his Son's parting without taking his Leave of them. He added, "He had a Buſineſs which required ſuch haſte, as would not ſuffer him a Minute's time at his diſpoſal." As to myſelf, Madam, I was comfortleſs, being inſenſible to every thing: And if any thing could eaſe me, 'twas ſome hours Converſation with my dear Henrietta, with whom I freely vented my thoughts touching the long Abſence of Mendez.

'In the mean time the Marqueſs de Los Rios was out of Danger, and my Father went often to ſee him: I obſerv'd one day great Alteration on my Mother's Countenance, ſhe and my Father having been long ſhut up with Religioſes, who came to give 'em a Viſit; and after a Conference of ſome time, they call'd me, without my being able to divine the Cauſe.

'I entred into their Apartment in ſuch Diſorder, that I knew not what I did. One of theſe good Fathers, Ven-

Venerable by his Age and Habit, spake much to me about the Resignation we owe to the Divine Will, on his Providence, in every thing which relates to us: and the Close of his Discourse was, that Mendez was taken by the Algerines; that he was a Slave; and by his Misfortune these Pyrates had learnt he was a rich Merchant's Son; which had occasion'd the setting him at an extraordinary Ransom: That they were at Algiers in the time he arriv'd; would have willingly brought him along with 'em, but the money which they had for all, was not sufficient for him alone. That at their Return they had been at his Father's to inform him of this vexatious Disaster; but found he had absented himself; and that the loss of a Galion, on which was embarkt all his Effects without being able to save any thing, had induced him to avoid his Creditors, who sought him every-where, to throw him in Prison: That things being in

Con-

Condition, they faw no Remedy to poor Mendez his Misfortunes, being in the hands of Meluza the moft famous and covetous of all the Corfaries; and that if I would follow their Advice, and that of my Parents, I would think of taking another Party. I had fo far heard this dreadful News in fo ecftatic a Condition, that I could only interrupt them by fad Sighs; but when he told me, I muft think of another Party; I burft out with Tears and Shrieks, as made both my Father and Mother, and thefe Religiofes compaffionate me.

'I was carried into my Chamber as one nearer death than life; and Donna Henrietta was fent for, and it was not without great Affliction fhe beheld me in this fad Condition. I fell into a moft deep Melancholly; I tormented myfelf day and night, and nothing was able to remove my dear Mendez out of my Mind.

'The Marquefs de Los Rios, having learnt

learnt what had paſt, conceiv'd ſuch ſtrong Hopes, that he ſoon found himſelf in a Condition to come and Claim of my Father and me the Effect of the Words we had given him. I ſhewed him that mine were not diſengaged in reſpect of Mendez; that he was Unfortunate, which no ways leſſen'd my Engagements to him. He heard me without being perſwaded by me, and told me, I had the ſame deſire of deſtroying myſelf, as others had of ſaving themſelves; that 'twas more my Intereſt than his, which made him act as he did. And being raviſht with having a Pretence which ſeemed to him plauſible, he preſt my Father with ſuch Earneſtneſs, that he at length conſented to what he deſired.

'It is impoſſible for me to repreſent to you, Madam, in what an Abyſs of Sorrow I was in: "What is become, my Lord," ſaid I to the Marqueſs, "of that ſcrupulous Tenderneſs which hinder'd you from taking my Heart from
any

any other hand than my own? Let me at leaſt have ſome time to forget Mendez; Perhaps his Abſence and Misfortunes may prevail on me to ſome Indifferency towards him. To this cruel Accident, which has ſnatch'd him ſo lately from me, you add new Troubles when you expect I ſhould ſo ſpeedily paſs over from him to you."

'"I know not what I expect or may hope for," ſaid he to me, "but this I am ſure of, that my Complaiſance had like to have coſt me my Life; that if you be not deſign'd for me, you will be anothers; and as to Mendez, his Fortune has been ſuch, that he can no longer pretend to you; and ſeeing you muſt be diſpoſed of, I think you are very hard hearted to refuſe me. You cannot be ignorant of what I have done hitherto to pleaſe you, my former Proceeding ſhould ſerve as a ſufficient Teſtimony of my future Reſpects."

'The Marqueſs made a greater pro-
grefs

grefs in my Father's Mind than mine. In a Word, my Mother having one day fent for me, told me, 'Twas to no purpofe to ufe any longer Delays, my Father being refolv'd I fhould obey his Orders. Whatever I could fay to excufe my felf, my Tears, my Remonftrances, Entreaties were all to no purpofe, and ferv'd only to exafperate my Mother.

' All things neceffary were prepared for my Marriage, the Marquefs would have every thing fuitable to his Quality; He fent me a Cabinet of Jewels and Precious Stones, to the value of feveral thoufand Crowns. The fatal Day for our Wedding was fet. Seeing my felf reduced to this Extremity. I took a refolution which will furprize you, Madam, and demonftrate a great Paffion.

'I went to Donna Henrietta; this Friend had been ever faithful to me, and threw my felf at her feet, furprifing her by fo extraordinary a Carriage:

"My

"My dear Henrietta," said I to her, melting in Tears, "there is no Remedy to my Misfortunes, unless you have pity on me; do not abandon me, let me conjure you in the sad Condition I am in; to morrow I must marry the Marquess de Los Rios, I can no longer avoid it. If the Offers of Friendship you have made me be Proof against all Tryal, and can make you capable of a generous Resolution, you will not refuse to follow my Fortune, and to accompany me to Algiers to pay Mendez his Ransom, to redeem him from the cruel Slavery he is in. You see me at your Feet," continued I, "I will never rise till you have given me your Word, to do what I desire you." She seem'd so concern'd at my Posture, that I arose to make her answer me. She immediately embraced me with great Testimonies of Tenderness: "I will refuse you nothing, my dear Mariana," said she to me, "were it my very Life; but you are going to ruine your self felf and me with you. How can two Girls execute what you project. Our Age, our Sex, and your Beauty, will expofe us to Accidents, the bare imagination of which makes me to tremble: this is certain, we are going to overwhelm our Families with Shame and Confufion; and if you had made ferious Reflections hereon, it is not poffible you could have come to this Refolution." "Ah, barbarous!" cried I, "and more barbarous than he that detains my Lover; you forfake me, but tho I am alone, yet that fhall not hinder me from purfuing my Point, neither can the affiftance you fhould give me ftand me in much ftead: Remain, remain, I confent, it is fit I fhould depart without any Comfort to affront all Dangers; I confefs fuch an undertaking is fit only for a defperate Creature."

'My Reproaches and Tears moved Henrietta; fhe told me my Intereft had obliged her as much as her own to
fpeak

speak to me as she had done; but in short, seeing I persisted in my first Resolution, and nothing could divert me from it, she resolved I should not go alone; That if I would be ruled by her, we should disguise ourselves; that she would undertake to get two Suits of Mens Apparel; and as for the rest, it belong'd to me to take care of it. I embraced her with a thousand Testimonies of Thankfulness.

'I afterwards askt her, Whether she had seen the Jewels which the Marquess had sent me; "I will bring them," said I to her, "to purchase Mendez's Ransom with them." We resolved to lose no time, and we neither of us fail'd in what we had projected.

'Never were two Maidens better disguised under the Habit of two Cavaliers. We parted that Night, and embarkt our selves without the least Obstacle, but after some days Sail we were overtaken by so violent a Storm,

as

as made us defpair of our Safety. In all this Diforder and Peril, I was lefs concerned for my felf, than for not having compaffed my dear Mendez's Liberty, and for having engaged Henrietta to follow my ill Fortune: "It is I," faid I to her, in embracing her, "it is I, my dear Companion, that has rais'd this Storm, were I not on the Sea it would be Calm; my Misfortune follows me wherever I go." In fine, we having been a Day and two Nights in continual Alarums, the Weather chang'd, and we arriv'd at Algiers.

'I was fo glad to fee my felf in a Condition to deliver Mendez, that I reckon'd all the Dangers we underwent as nothing: But alas, what became of me in difembarking, when after all the fearch which could be made, I perceiv'd there was no hope of finding the little Cabinet wherein I had put all I had was moft precious: I found my felf feiz'd with fuch violent Grief, that I thought I fhould have expired

pired before I got out of the Vessel. Without doubt this Cabinet, which was little, and of which I took but small Care during the Tempest, fell into the Sea, or was stole, which ever of these two it was, I made a considerable Loss, and I had only remaining Jewels to the value of a thousand Pounds, which I had kept for all Events about me.

'I resolv'd with this, to make a Tryal with Mendez's Patron: As soon as we were in the Town, we enquired out his House, (for Meluza was well known) and went thither clad as Gentlemen.

'I cannot express to you, Madam, the trouble I was in drawing near this House, where I knew my dear Lover languisht in Chains; what sad Reflections did I not make; how did I look when I enter'd the Corsary's House, and saw Mendez Chain'd, with several others, who were leading out to work in the Field. I should have fallen at his

his Feet, had not Henrietta born me up: I no longer knew where I was, nor what I did; I would have spoken to him, but Grief had so seiz'd on my Spirits, that my Tongue could not utter a Word. As to him, he beheld me not; he was so sad and deprest, that he could look on no body; and one must love him as much as I did, to know him, so greatly was he changed.

'After having been some time coming to my self, I went into a low Room, where I was told Meluza was; I saluted him, and told him the occasion of my Voyage; that Mendez was my near Relation; that he was undone by the Loss of a Galion, and his Captivity together; and that 'twas out of my own Money I would pay his Ransom. The Moor appear'd to me little concern'd at what I said; and looking scornfully on me, he answer'd, It was not his business to enquire whence I had my Money; but this he he certainly knew, that Mendez was Rich; and to ſhew that he would not take all Advantages, he would therefore ſet him at twenty thouſand Crowns.

'Alas, what would this have been, had I not loſt my Jewels? but this was too much in the Condition I was in. In fine, after ſeveral long fruitleſs Diſputes, I took on me immediately a reſolution which could only be inſpired by an extream Love.

'"Here's all I have," ſaid I to the Pyrate, in giving him my Diamonds, "they are not worth what thou demandeſt: take me for thy Slave, and be perſwaded thou wilt not keep me long. I am the only Daughter of a Rich Banker of Seville; keep me for an Hoſtage, and let Mendez go; he will ſoon return to Redeem me." The Barbarian was ſurpriz'd to find me capable of ſo generous and affectionate a Reſolution. "Thou art worthy," ſaid he to me, "of a better Fortune. Be

Be it fo; I accept the Condition you offer me: I will take care of thee, and be a good Patron to thee. Thou muft leave the Habit thou weareft, to put on one agreeable to thy Sex: thou fhalt keep thy Jewels if thou wilt, I can as well ftay for the whole as for a part."

'Donna Henrietta was fo confufed and difmayed at the Bargain I came from concluding, that fhe could not fufficiently exprefs her Difpleafure to me; but in fine, maugre all her Remonftrances and Entreaties, I held firm, and Meluza caus'd a Slave's Habit to be brought me, which I put on.

'He conducted me to his Wives Chamber, to whom he deliver'd me, having recounted to her what I had done for my Lover's Liberty.

'She feem'd to be much affected by it, and promis'd fhe would fhorten the time of my Servitude by all the good Treatments fhe could make me.

'At Night, when Mendez return'd, Meluza

Meluza caus'd him to be call'd, telling him, That being of Seville, he would therefore fhew him a Slave he had bought, becaufe perhaps he might know her.

'Immediately I was brought before him; Mendez at this fight, lofing all Countenance, came and caſt himfelf at my Feet, and taking my Hands, which he bathed with his Tears, he faid every thing which was moſt tender and affectionate to me. Meluza and his Wife diverted themfelves, in feeing the different Motions of Joy and Grief with which we were agitated: in fine, they inform'd Mendez of the Obligations he had to me; that he was free, and that I would remain in his place. He did whatever could be done to diffwade me from taking this Task on me: "Alas," faid he to me, "you would have me load you with my Chains, my dear Miſtreſs; Shall I be free, when you are not? I go then to do for you what you come from

doing

doing for me; I will fell my felf, and Redeem you with this Money: for in fine, confider, that fhould I as foon as I arrive at Seville, find Affiftance, and return again to bring you back, yet how is it poffible for me in the mean time to leave you; judge how I can do this in a time wherein my Fortune promifes me nothing, and am the moft Unhappy of all Men." I offered againft all his Reafons, the Tendernefs of my Father, who would foon Redeem me when he knew where I was. In fine, I made ufe of all the Power I had over his Mind, to make his Advantage of what I had done in his Favour.

'What fhall I fay to you, Madam, of our Separation? It was fo dolorous, that Words cannot exprefs what we felt. I obliged Henrietta to part with him, to follicite and prefs my Parents to do their part in my behalf.

'In the mean time my Father and Mother were in an unconceivable Affliction; and when they perceiv'd
my

my flight they thought to die with Grief.

'They blamed themſelves infinitely for forcing me to marry the Marqueſs de Los Reos. He was for his part in no leſs Deſpair; they cauſed me to be ſearcht for in vain, in all places where they thought I might have hid my ſelf.

'Two whole Years were paſt without my receiving any News or Succors from Mendez; which made me believe with great likelihood, that both he and Henrietta were caſt away on the Sea: I had given them all the Jewels which Meluza had left me; but it was not their Loſs, nor that of my Liberty, which I regretted: It was of my dear Lover and faithful Friend, whoſe Remembrance continually poſſeſt me, and caus'd me an unparallel'd Affliction; I could get no Reſt nor Health; I wept Day and Night; I refuſed to come out of my Slavery in neglecting to ſignifie to my Father my preſent Condition. I wiſht only

only for a speedy Death, which I would have willingly met with, to put an end to my Troubles and Misfortunes.

'Meluza and his Wife began to pity me: they did not doubt but Mendez was cast away: they treated me less cruelly than these sort of People are wont to use those Unhappy Wretches who fall into their Hands.

'One Day, as Meluza came from Pyrating, he brought with him several Persons of both Sexes which he had taken, and among the rest a Young Woman of some Quality of Seville, and whom I knew. This sight renewed my Grief: she was much surpriz'd to find me in this sad place. We affectionately embraced one another, and observing a deep silence; "How now, Beautiful Mariana," said she to me, "are you so indifferent towards your Relations and Country, that you have no Curiosity to make any Enquiries about them?" I lifted up mine

mine Eyes to Heaven in uttering a deep Sigh; I entreated her to tell me, If 'twere known where Mendez and Henrietta were loſt? "Who has told you they are loſt?" replied ſhe. "They are at Seville, where they lead a very happy Life. Mendez has re-eſtabliſht his Affairs, and makes it his great Delight and Honour to publiſh in all places the Extream Obligations he has to Henrietta. Perhaps you are ignorant," continued ſhe, "that Mendez was taken and made a Slave by the Algerines; this generous young Woman diſguiſed her ſelf, and came hither to redeem him, but he has not been ungrateful, for he has married her. There is a moſt charming Union between them. Hymen has not baniſht Love in their particular."

'As ſhe was yet ſpeaking, ſhe perceiv'd my Countenance to alter on a a ſudden, and that I was ready to faint; my Strength fail'd me, mine Eyes cloſed, and I ſunk down between her

her Arms; fhe was greatly troubled at this; fhe called my Companions, who put me to Bed, and endeavour'd to recover me from this pitious Condition.

'This young Woman greatly concern'd her felf for me; and when I came to my felf, I began to complain; I uttered Sighs and Groans able to move a Rock.

'Meluza was affected at the Recital of fuch a worfe than barbarous Inftance of Treachery, and without any notice to me, he inform'd himfelf, by his new Slave of my Father's Name, and immediately wrote to him what he knew of my Misfortunes.

'Thefe Letters were like to have been the Death of my Mother; fhe could not imagine I could be in Chains at eighteen Years of Age, without fhedding a torrent of Tears: But that which augmented her Grief, was, the Diforder of my Father's Affairs; feveral confiderable Bankrupts had ruined him; his Credit was gone, and it was
im-

impoſſible for him to procure the 20000 Crowns which Meluza demanded for my Ranſom.

'The Generous Marqueſs de Los Rios heard this News, came to my Father, and offered him what lay in his Power: "I do not do this," ſaid he, "in deſign to force your Daughter's Inclinations when ſhe ſhall be here; I ſhall love her always, but I will never diſpleaſe her." My Father having no other way of Relief, thankfully accepted of what was offered him; and in a word, embarkt himſelf, and happily arriv'd at Argiers, in the time when I thought only of dying.

'He forbore all thoſe Reproaches I deſerv'd; he redeem'd me, and at my Intreaty, this young Woman of Seville, for a moderate Ranſom. We return'd together, and my Mother receiv'd me with ſuch joy as is impoſſible to be expreſt. I anſwer'd hereto as much as was poſſible; but I carried always

in

in my Heart, Madam, the fatal Stroke which had wounded me: Whatever my Reaſon could repreſent to me, was not ſufficient to Eface out of my Remembrance the Image of the Traitor Mendez.

'I ſaw the Marqueſs de Los Rios: he dared not mention the Inclinations he ſtill had towards me; but I had ſuch preſſing Obligations to him, that Gratitude made me do for him, what my Inclinations would have made me do for another.

'I gave him my Hand, and he his to me, with ſuch Affection, as if he had had no ſolid Matter of Complaint againſt me.

'In fine, I married him, and apprehending leſt I ſhould ſee Mendez, that Ungrateful Wretch, to whom I owe ſuch Horrour, and for whom I had ſo little, I pray'd the Marqueſs we might dwell in the Country-houſe he had near Seville.

'He ever approv'd of what I liked;
he

he would have my Father and Mother retire; he lefs'ned the fad Condition of their Fortune, by confiderable Liberalities: and I may truly fay, there never was a greater Soul. Judge, Madam, of all the Reproaches I made my Heart for its not being fo tender to him as it ought to have been: It was not in my power to forget Mendez, and I always felt new Regrets, when I learnt his Felicity with the Unfaithful Henrietta.

'Having paft two Years in a continual watching over myfelf, that I might do nothing but what was agreeable to my Husband, Heaven depriv'd me of him, of this Generous Husband; and he did for me in thefe laft Moments, what he had already heretofore done, giving me all he had, with fuch Teftimonies of Efteem and Affection, as much enhanced the Price of the Gift: He made me the richeft Widow of Andaloufia, but he could not make me the Happieft.

'I

'I would not return to Seville, where my Parents would have had me been; and to avoid it, I pretended a Journey farther into the Country, to look after some part of my Estate. I set out; but there being a particular Fatality in whatever relates to me, in arriving at an Inn, the first Object which struck my sight, was the Unfaithful Mendez: he was in deep Mourning, and had lost nothing of whatever made me heretofore fancy him too Lovely. It is impossible to express the Condition I was in, for endeavouring to get speedily from him, I found myself so weak and trembling, that I fell at his Feet. Although he knew me not that instant, yet he earnestly endeavour'd to raise me up; but the great Veil under which I was conceal'd, flying open, what became of him in seeing me? He remain'd no less confused than I was: he would have drawn near to me, but casting a furious Look on him: "Darest thou, Perjured Wretch!" said I to him,

him, "dareſt thou approach me! Art thou not afraid of the juſt Puniſhment of thy Perfidiouſneſs?" He was ſome time without anſwering me, and I was about leaving him when he ſtopt me: "Confound and overwhelm me with Reproaches, Madam," ſaid he to me: "Give me the worſt and moſt perfidious Names as is poſſible; they cannot be more than I deſerve: but my Death ſhall ſoon revenge your Quarrel: I ought to die with Sorrow for having betray'd you; and if I regret any thing in dying, it is only the having one Life to loſe, to expiate all the Crimes you can juſtly accuſe me of." He appear'd to me much affected in ending theſe words; and would to Heavens his Repentance were really ſufficient and true! I would not hazard a longer Converſation with him: I left him, diſdaining to return him an Anſwer. And this Mark of Contempt and Slighting, was, without doubt, more ſenſible to him, than

than all the Reproaches I might have made him.

'He had some time since lost his Wife, that Unfaithful Creature, who had helpt him to Revolt against all the Offices of Love, Honour, and Gratitude. And from that time he follow'd me every-where: he was like a Complaining Shadow, ever fastned to my Feet; for he became so lean, pale, and chang'd, that he was no longer discernable. Heavens! Madam, what Violence did I not offer myself, in continuing to ill Treat him: I found at last I wanted Strength to resist the Weakness of my Heart, and the Ascendant this Wretch had over me. Rather than to commit so shameful an offence, and to Forgive him, I parted for Madrid, where I have Relations, and sought among them a Shelter against the Violence of mine own Inclinations.

'I was not there long but Mendez found me out: I must confess to you,

I was not heartily difpleas'd at his Attendance on me; but maugre my Inclinations towards him, I put on a firm Refolution to avoid him, feeing I could not fincerely hate him; and unknown to every Body, I took the Road to Burgos, where I am going to Cloyfter myfelf with a Religious there, my Friend. I flatter myfelf, Madam, with the Hopes of finding more Reft there, than I have hitherto met with.'

The Beautiful Marchionefs here held her peace; and I testified to her my particular Acknowledgments for the Favour fhe had done me: I affured her of the part I took in her Adventures: I conjured her to write to me, and let me hear from her at Madrid; and fhe promifed it me in the moft obliging Manner as is poffible.

We found the next Morning we could not fet out, it having fnow'd all the Night, and no Path appearing on the Ground; but we wanted not Company to pafs the time in Play and
Dif-

Difcourfe. Having been three days with the Marchionefs de Los Rios, without any Wearinefs at the length of the Time, through the pleafure I had of feeing and hearing her talk (for fhe is one of the moft lovely Women in the World:) We parted with a mutual Regret, and it was not without doubling our Promifes of writing to, and feeing one another hereafter.

The Weather mended, and I continued on my Journey to Lerma: We had traverft dreadful Mountains, which bear the Name of Sierra de Cogollos, and it was not without great trouble we got thither: This Town is fmall; fhe has given her name to the famous Cardinal de Lerma, Chief Minifter to Philip III: it is from him that Philip IV. took the great Revenues he had receiv'd from the King his Mafter. Here is a Caftle which I will fee to Morrow, and of which I fhall give you an Account in my next. I am told an Extraordinary Exprefs is arriv'd, and will

will fet out to Night: I will lay hold of this Opportunity of fending to you, and ending this long Letter; for in truth I am tired both with the Way, and with Writing, but I fhall never be weary of Loving you.

From Lerma,
   Mar. 5, 1679.

FINIS.

Reprinted for
Archer M. Huntington
At the Knickerbocker Press
G. P. Putnam's Sons
1899

www.ingramcontent.com/pod-product-compliance
Lightning Source LLC
Chambersburg PA
CBHW032059220426
43664CB00008B/1070